Cambridge English

Complete First for Schools

Workbook with answers with Audio CD

Barbara Thomas

Amanda Thomas

with Helen Tiliouine

Cambridge University Press
www.cambridge.org/elt

Cambridge English Language Assessment
www.cambridgeenglish.org

Information on this title: www.cambridge.org/9781107656345

© Cambridge University Press 2014

This publication is in copyright. Subject to statutory exception
and to the provisions of relevant collective licensing agreements,
no reproduction of any part may take place without the written
permission of Cambridge University Press.

First published 2014
20 19 18 17 16 15 14 13 12 11 10 9 8 7 6 5

Printed in Dubai by Oriental Press

A catalogue record for this publication is available from the British Library

ISBN 978-1-107-67516-2 Student's Book without answers with CD-ROM
ISBN 978-1-107-66159-2 Student's Book with answers with CD-ROM
ISBN 978-1-107-68336-5 Teacher's Book
ISBN 978-1-107-67179-9 Workbook without answers with Audio CD
ISBN 978-1-107-65634-5 Workbook with answers with Audio CD
ISBN 978-1-107-69533-7 Class Audio CDs (2)
ISBN 978-1-107-68529-1 Presentation Plus DVD-ROM

The publishers have no responsibility for the persistence or accuracy of URLs
for external or third-party internet websites referred to in this publication, and
do not guarantee that any content on such websites is, or will remain, accurate
or appropriate. Information regarding prices, travel timetables, and other
factual information given in this work is correct at the time of first printing but
the publishers do not guarantee the accuracy of such information thereafter.

Contents

1	A family affair	4
2	Leisure and pleasure	8
3	Happy holidays?	12
4	Food, glorious food	16
5	Study time	20
6	My first job	24
7	High adventure	28
8	Dream of the stars	32
9	Secrets of the mind	36
10	On the money	40
11	Medical matters	44
12	Animal kingdom	48
13	House space	52
14	Fiesta!	56

Answer key	60
Acknowledgements	80

A family affair

Grammar

Present perfect simple and continuous

1 Read this email and put the verbs in brackets into the most appropriate form (present perfect simple or continuous).

To: Stephanie

Hi Stephanie
How are you? I **(1)** _'ve been having_ (have) a lovely time with my family here in Spain. Sorry I **(2)** .... (not write) to you for ages, but I **(3)** .... (work) hard here at my new school since we arrived six weeks ago. My new teachers are all great and I **(4)** .... (meet) some really nice Spanish people. Some of them **(5)** .... (invite) me round to their houses a few times. I think my Spanish **(6)** .... (improve) a lot because I **(7)** .... (not have) the opportunity to speak much English since I arrived, except to my family. It's hard having all my lessons in Spanish instead of English, but I'll get used to it. It's lucky my mum's Spanish and made sure we all learnt the language as we were growing up! She **(8)** .... (go) to Madrid this weekend to stay with her sister, so Dad's looking after us all. His mum, my English grandmother, is missing us a lot – she **(9)** .... (phone) six times already! I **(10)** .... (look after) my little brother and sister this morning to help Dad. They **(11)** .... (play) in the garden since breakfast though and they're quite happy so I **(12)** .... (write) emails all morning. I **(13)** .... (send) six so far!
I **(14)** .... (wonder) what you **(15)** .... (do) since I left! Write back soon and tell me all your news.
Love Emily

Asking questions (present perfect simple and continuous)

2 A week later, Stephanie phones Emily and asks her some questions. Use the prompts to write her questions using the most appropriate form (present perfect simple or continuous) in the speech balloons.

1 you visit / Madrid yet?

   Have you visited Madrid yet?

2 What time / you get up / every day?

3 you buy / anything?

4 you learn / how to cook Spanish food?

5 How many times / you eat / paella?

6 you see / any films in Spanish yet?

Vocabulary

Collocations with *make* and *do*

1 (EP) Complete each of the sentences below with the correct form of *make* or *do*.

1 Don't worry about the exam. You can only ...*do*... your best.
2 Carla dropped a whole bottle of olive oil and it .... a mess.
3 Everyone was asleep when I came home so I tried not to .... a noise.
4 My mum says I can .... a swimming course for a week this summer.
5 I needed to have my hair cut so Dad rang the hairdresser to .... an appointment for me.
6 I often help my parents .... the shopping.
7 I missed school on Monday because I was ill so my friend .... a copy of all the notes for me.
8 The sink was full of dirty dishes so I .... the washing up.
9 I've been given some money for my birthday, but I'm not sure whether to buy a computer game or some new trousers. It's difficult to .... a decision!
10 My mum is going to .... a delicious meal for us when we get home.

Adjectives

2 (EP) For each of the sentences below, make an adjective from one of the words in the box. Some gaps need a negative adjective.

> aggression criticism enthusiasm organise
> patience rely understand

1 My aunt can be quite ...*critical*... when I make mistakes but she always gives me good advice too.
2 Although Charlie wanted to see the show, he was too .... to stand in the queue for half an hour.
3 Most animals will get .... if they feel their young are being threatened.
4 Mark's family are so .... they can never find anything they need.
5 When Petra explained why she was late, her teacher was very .... and didn't get angry.
6 Stacey is really .... She promises to do things but often changes her mind.
7 I thought you'd be really excited about going to Amsterdam but you don't seem very ....

Phrasal verbs

3 (EP) Complete each gap with a phrasal verb which means the same as the word(s) in brackets. Use the verbs in the box in their correct form.

> clear up ~~do up~~ go for go on pick up wear out

When my cousin comes to stay in the holidays she shares my room. Last summer I thought I'd give her a surprise and (1) ...*do it up*... (*decorate it*) before she came. First of all, I had to (2) .... (*tidy*) and that took ages because it was a real mess. In fact, I was so (3) .... (*tired*) that I had to have a rest before going to the shop to buy the paint. I couldn't decide whether to (4) .... (*choose*) green or blue but in the end blue seemed best. When I came out of the shop, I realised I couldn't carry all the stuff I'd bought so my mum had to come and (5) .... (*collect me*). Then I only had a day to get it all done. I (6) .... (*continue*) painting nearly all night. The annoying thing was my cousin didn't even notice when she arrived.

Writing Part 2 — An article

Read part of an article written by a student for a magazine and correct the spelling and punctuation. There are 15 mistakes. The first one has been corrected for you.

Being a teenager

I ~~definately~~ *definitely* think that teenage year's should be the best in everyones life because you can have fun and you have fewer problems than adults teenagers know how to have a good time. Most teenagers have a lot of freinds and they discuss things that they are interested in. Teenagers have to be in fashion wearing up-to-date cloths and listening to modern music. They also like to do sports and compete in matchs. But teenager's parents sometimes have a difficult time and they dont understand why? Wouldnt you feel angry if someone went into your room without permission. So do teenagers. Teenagers stop thinking like children as they grow up and their believes and their interests change. My opinion is that teenage years are magical and Id like to stay a teenager forever.

Unit 1

Listening Part 3

▶02 You will hear five short extracts in which teenagers are talking about a family day out. For questions 1–5, choose from the list (A–H) what each speaker says about the day. Use the letters only once. There are three extra letters which you do not need to use.

A I got bored with what we were doing after a while.
B I enjoyed the day more than I had expected.
C I had a better time than some members of my family.
D I was disappointed about something.
E I was annoyed about a change of plan.
F I didn't have time to do everything I wanted.
G I regretted a decision I made.
H I was relieved that the day was a success.

Speaker 1 [ ] 1
Speaker 2 [ ] 2
Speaker 3 [ ] 3
Speaker 4 [ ] 4
Speaker 5 [ ] 5

EXAM ADVICE

Read A–H and listen carefully to each speaker. The words you hear will be different from those below.

Reading and Use of English Part 7

You are going to read a newspaper article about people who have no brothers or sisters. For questions 1–10, choose from the people (A–E). The people may be chosen more than once.

EXAM ADVICE

Read the questions, then quickly read the texts. When you find the part of a text which matches the question, underline it.

Which person

realises that the positive relationship they had with their parents isn't shared by all only children?	1
thinks people make a judgement about only children which is mistaken?	2
thinks they developed a better understanding of adults because of being an only child?	3
finds their present circumstances a challenge?	4
says that only children have needs which can be difficult for others to deal with?	5
realised at a particular point that they were happy being an only child?	6
was unaware that their reactions to being an only child were not unique?	7
had problems as a child because they lacked a necessary skill?	8
says they accept their situation because they don't know anything different?	9
mentions a positive benefit of spending a lot of time alone?	10

Being an only child

"What's it like to spend a lifetime without brothers and sisters?" asks Joanna Moorhead.

A   Sam Thompson, aged 10

When my mum's friend had a baby, it made me think about being an only child for the first time. I thought, would I like to have brothers and sisters? But to be honest, my friend's sister looked quite annoying – he was always having to watch her and I decided I was better off on my own. There are lots of good things about being an only child. I have privacy, and I like that; some of my friends have to share a bedroom and I know that will never happen to me. Plus I get time on my own with Mum and Dad, and that's very special.

B   Jasmine Weller, aged 13

I always felt a bit different from other kids, and just thought it was something about me. Then I made friends with three other people who are all only children. I suddenly realised that they felt a lot like me. We all need to spend quite a lot of time on our own, and some of our friends with brothers and sisters find that strange – they think we don't like them or something. However, there are pluses, too. I think it's good to be able to entertain yourself sometimes, and my mum says I've got a great imagination.

C   Bethany Shaw, aged 15

One of the bad things about being an only child when you're young is the reaction you get from other people. They think you're spoilt – you see that look in their eyes. And then you have to prove you're not spoilt, although you know you're not and nor are most only children. In general, I think the negatives outweigh the positives, but on the other hand it's all I've known and I'm OK with it.

D   Leah Mitchell, aged 29

I went away to school when I was seven, and the hardest thing I found was making friends. Because I was an only child, I just didn't know how to do it. The thing is that when you're an only child, often there aren't any other children at a gathering. I found being an only child interesting, in that it gave me a place at the grown-ups' table and gave me a view into their world that children in a big family might not get. And I know it has, at least partly, made me into the person I am: I never like the idea of being one of a group, for example. I'm not comfortable with being one of a gang.

E   Laura Arnold, aged 36

I know some only children feel stifled by their parents' constant demands and worries, but that wasn't my experience. I found being an only child enriching, which I think is mainly because we get on so well. I've got two children now and I do find that scary. The problem is I've absolutely no experience of this kind of situation; nothing in my past has prepared me for having to divide myself between the needs of these two little people, and the guilt is hard when I feel I've not been there enough for one of them. And on a practical level, things like sibling rivalry are going to be a whole new ball game.

2 Leisure and pleasure

Grammar
Making comparisons

1 Circle the correct comparative form.

1 I think people's health is getting *more and more* / (*better and better*) these days.
2 The *most* / *more* hard-working people I know are my grandparents. They're always busy in the house or in the garden.
3 The *riskier* / *riskiest* sport I've tried is mountain biking.
4 Learning to play the piano is *much more* / *much* harder than I thought.
5 He doesn't play chess nearly as *well* / *good* as his brother.
6 I get *less* / *the least* pocket money from my parents every week than my older brother.
7 You're *more* / *far* better at basketball than me because you practise more.
8 He's the *least* / *less* sporty person I know.

2 Some of these sentences contain mistakes. Correct the mistakes and put a tick (✓) next to the sentences which are correct.

1 Practising every day is the ~~better~~ *best* way to learn an instrument.
2 Golf is the least enjoyable sport to watch on TV. ✓
3 Tennis is the more hardest sport to learn.
4 Riding a motorbike is more fun than taking the bus!
5 It's less easier to learn a new sport as you get older.
6 For me, playing computer games is the more relaxing way to spend my free time.
7 Joining a sports club can help people to become more healthier.
8 I am the fittest now than I have ever been in my life.

Adjectives with -ed and -ing

3 Complete the words to form adjectives with *-ed* or *-ing*.

1 He's an amaz............... person; he's not afraid to do anything.
2 Joseph can be really irritat............... when he's in a silly mood.
3 I'm not interest............... in learning to drive.
4 It was really embarrass............... . I burnt all the sausages when my friends came over for a barbecue.
5 I was quite disappoint............... not to win the tennis match, after I'd trained so hard.
6 I don't find computer games at all relax............... .

4 Complete the table with the verb and noun forms.

Adjective	Verb	Noun
amused / amusing	*to amuse*	
confused / confusing		
embarrassed / embarrassing		
exhaust / exhausting		
excited / exciting		
relaxed / relaxing		
shocked / shocking		
worried / worrying		

Leisure and pleasure

Writing Part 2

Organising ideas into paragraphs
Compound and complex sentences

1 Read the sentences about a children's game. Make complex sentences by joining the two sentences in each line with *and*, *but* or *because*.

1 I enjoy playing it with all my friends. It's really exciting.

2 Any number of people can play. It's more fun with between six and eight players.

3 My favourite game is called 'Pom Pom Home'. I have been playing it since I was five.

4 During the holidays we play for hours. We get home completely exhausted.

5 To rescue someone you have to run and touch 'home'. Then you have to run away quickly before you get caught.

6 It's basically quite similar to 'Hide and Seek'. It's a bit more complicated and active.

7 I love it when my big brother plays with us. He's a fast runner and he always rescues me if I get caught.

8 It's different every time we play. There are so many places where we can hide.

2 Now look at the exam task and a student's plan below. Match the combined sentences (1–8) from a student's answer to the correct paragraphs (A–C).

This month's writing competition:
Children's games
What was your favourite game when you were a child?
Tell us:
· How to play the game
· Why you enjoyed it
The winning article will be published next month.

Student's plan

A Paragraph 1: Introduction – a brief description of the game and when you played it
Sentences ....3............ ....

B Paragraph 2: How to play the game
Sentences ....

C Paragraph 3: Why you enjoyed it
Sentences ....

Vocabulary

Phrasal verbs with *up*

1 **EP** Which of these things can you *take up*, *start up*, *sum up* and *make up*? Write the words under the correct phrasal verb.

an offer   ~~a hobby~~
a story   a business   a machine
the main points of an argument
a sport   an excuse

take up	start up	make up	sum up
a hobby			

Unit 2

Phrasal verbs with off

2 EP Match the phrasal verbs with their definitions.

1 go off
2 put off
3 let someone off
4 show off
5 set off
6 cut off

A start a journey
B explode
C excuse someone from doing something
D interrupt a power supply
E postpone
F boast

3 Complete each sentence with the correct form of one of the phrasal verbs in Exercise 2.

1 We cycled to the swimming pool but it was closed so we ……set off…… for the park instead.
2 As soon as they heard the burglar alarm ………………… , the thieves drove off in their waiting car.
3 She's always ………………… about how good she is at gymnastics.
4 The lights aren't working. I think the electricity has been ………………… .
5 We didn't have to do the test again because the teacher ………………… .
6 The match was ………………… until the next day because of the rain.

Listening Part 4

EXAM INFORMATION

In Listening Part 4, there are seven questions and you choose one answer from three possible options. You hear the recording twice.

▶03 You will hear part of a radio interview with Toby Lucas, a young chess player. For questions 1–7, choose the best answer (A, B or C).

1 Toby joined his chess club because
   A he wanted to play in tournaments with a successful team.
   B he knew there were a lot of good players there.
   C he wanted to meet players of his own age.

2 Why did Toby stop playing chess on the Internet?
   A He needed a greater range of players.
   B His chess wasn't progressing.
   C It had never really appealed to him.

3 What does Toby like about his favourite grandmaster?
   A He takes risks.
   B He doesn't mind losing.
   C He always stays calm.

4 When deciding which move to make, Toby usually chooses
   A the one that feels right.
   B an aggressive move.
   C one that he planned before the game.

5 What does Toby say about becoming a top professional player?
   A He needs to work very hard to succeed as a professional.
   B He would enjoy playing professionally.
   C He thinks he lacks the necessary qualities to be a professional.

6 Playing chess has taught Toby to
   A be a more confident person.
   B understand people better.
   C control his body language.

7 According to Toby, how is life different to chess?
   A In chess it is easier to predict what's going to happen.
   B You don't need to plan life ahead as much.
   C In chess you have more choices.

Reading and Use of English Part 2

For questions **1–8**, read the text below and think of the word which best fits each gap. Use only **one** word in each gap. There is an example at the beginning (0).

Singing in a choir

The benefits **(0)** ...*of*... singing in a choir are numerous. Research has shown that young people **(1)** .... sing in choirs do better **(2)** .... their studies and have a tendency to be healthier. If you are considering joining a choir, you need to be sure that you can sing in tune. This might seem obvious, but unless you can, **(3)** .... is little point in seeking out a choir **(4)** .... you'll only get rejected. Any choir you apply **(5)** .... join is likely to want to audition you. Don't worry if you can't read music; that can **(6)** .... taught later. If you're accepted, you'll find choir practices hard work, but great fun. You'll learn how to read music and how to sing **(7)** .... confidence. Your voice and technique will probably develop quite quickly and you may just end **(8)** .... being one of the best singers at your school.

Reading and Use of English Part 4

For questions **1–6**, complete the second sentence so that it has a similar meaning to the first sentence, using the word given. **Do not change the word given.** You must use between **two** and **five** words, including the word given. Here is an example (0).

Example:

0 His sister plays chess better than he does.
AS
He doesn't play chess ......*as well as*...... his sister.

Write **only** the missing words **IN CAPITAL LETTERS**.

1 The ticket was cheaper than I had expected.
AS
The ticket ....
I had expected.

2 Eliza felt disappointed not to be chosen for the team.
FOR
It .... Eliza not to be chosen for the team.

3 Taking regular exercise is how my grandmother lived to be 100.
BECAUSE
My grandmother lived to be 100 ....
.... regular exercise.

4 She prefers tennis to hockey.
MUCH
She doesn't ....
as tennis.

5 I think golf is more boring than any other sport.
LEAST
I think golf ....
sport.

6 I was really excited during the race because I knew I was going to come first.
FOUND
I ....
because I knew I was going to come first.

3 Happy holidays?

Grammar

Past simple, past continuous, past perfect simple and past perfect continuous

1 Read these sentences about an overnight train journey from London to Switzerland and put the verbs in brackets into the past simple or the past continuous.

1 By the time the train ....*left*........ (leave), it ....*was getting*........ (get) dark.
2 We .... (still look) for our seats when the train .... (stop) for the first time.
3 We .... (meet) a family from Scotland, who .... (go) to a wedding in France.
4 In the evening, we .... (sit) in the buffet. We .... (not eat) much but we .... (talk) to some interesting people.
5 When I .... (wake up) in the morning, we .... (travel) through the vineyards.
6 As soon as we .... (cross) the border, I .... (begin) to feel excited.
7 When we .... (reach) the mountains, we .... (know) our journey was almost over.
8 The train .... (arrive) late and our friends .... (not wait) for us so we .... (take) a taxi to their flat.

2 For each gap, choose a verb from the box and put it into the past perfect or the past perfect continuous.

| feel forget own stand up try ~~wait~~ |

1 The crowd ....*had been waiting*........ for over an hour for the match to begin.
2 We .... to find the key for five minutes when my dad found it in his pocket.
3 When he retired, my grandfather .... his business for more than 40 years.
4 David .... unwell for a few days so he went to the doctor's.
5 Katrina was really angry with me because I .... to tell her the change of plan.
6 I was quite tired when I got home as I .... watching our school football team for over an hour.

3 For each gap, put the verb in brackets into the past simple, past continuous, past perfect simple or past perfect continuous.

Last week I **(1)** ....*went*........ (go) to the mountains with my cousins. None of us **(2)** .... (ever ski) before so we **(3)** .... (look) forward to it for months. While we **(4)** .... (drive) to the airport, it **(5)** .... (start) to snow and we were really excited. But when we **(6)** .... (get) off the plane in the mountains, there **(7)** .... (not be) any snow at all. Everyone there **(8)** .... (say) it was too warm for snow. We **(9)** .... (go) to bed feeling sad that we wouldn't be able to ski. But when we **(10)** .... (get) up the next morning and **(11)** .... (look) out of the window we realised that it **(12)** .... (snow) all night and we would be able to ski after all.

at, in and on in time phrases

4 Complete each gap in the email with *at*, *in* or *on*.

Dear Antonio
I'm glad you're visiting me and my family **(1)** ...*in*... the summer, but my parents say it's better if you come **(2)** .... August rather than September because I start school again **(3)** .... 6th September. I'm so looking forward to the holidays. I have to get up early **(4)** .... weekdays in term time because the bus to school leaves **(5)** .... 7.30. But I get up late **(6)** .... Saturdays and **(7)** .... the afternoon I meet my friends. I always play football **(8)** .... Sunday mornings so I get up quite early then too. **(9)** .... the holidays I spend a lot of time on the beach. Sometimes my family doesn't go to bed till quite late **(10)** .... night as it's really hot here and it's hard to get to sleep.
Can't wait to see you again.
Luke

Vocabulary

Suffixes

1 **EP** Make adjectives from the nouns in brackets.
1 My teacher is usually very ...*friendly*... but she can be strict sometimes too. (*friend*)
2 Keep away from that .... snake. (*poison*)
3 My father does .... research. (*science*)
4 My parents think skateboarding is .... , but I don't. (*risk*)
5 I don't think that wearing .... clothes makes you cool. I think your personality is more important. (*fashion*)
6 The children are so .... (*energy*)
7 The film had a very .... ending. (*drama*)
8 My family aren't very .... when we go on holiday. (*adventure*)
9 I live near a big .... city. (*industry*)
10 Ali is very selfish and .... (*thought*)
11 Adam is very .... and always wants to be the best at everything. (*competition*)
12 It's .... to feel a bit worried before a long journey abroad. (*nature*)

Travel words

2 **EP** Complete the crossword puzzle.

Across
4 I enjoyed trying different watersports on our .... holiday.
6 Sometimes my parents let me stay at my best friend's house ....
10 Before people flew, they had to make long .... across the sea to get from Europe to America.
11 My parents say that air .... has become much cheaper than it was when they were young.

Down
1 .... is very popular with young people who want to see the world.
2 I was really excited when we got to the airport and didn't even mind when our .... was delayed for an hour.
3 On Vancouver waterfront in Canada, you see lots of .... ships which are going to Alaska.
5 I've never been on a really long train .... , but I'd love to when I'm older.
7 When my sister and her friend went to Scotland, they stayed in youth ....
8 We didn't have much time so my parents decided we should go on a sightseeing .... with a guide.
9 My dad took a wrong turning on our .... home and we got lost.
11 The round .... from home to the supermarket and back took three hours because of the traffic. I wish I hadn't gone with my parents!

Unit 3

Word formation

3 Make adjectives from the words in **bold** in the left-hand column and put them in the correct columns in the table below. One example has been done for you.

	-y	-ible	-ic	-ful	-ive	-able	-al	-ious
colour				colourful				
respond								
storm								
mystery								
mass								
doubt								
emotion								
wealth								
access								
predict								

4 Replace the underlined words in the following sentences with a word from the table.

1 I'm <u>not sure</u> that he will succeed in beating the school 100 metre record.
2 They must be very <u>rich</u>, because they own some valuable paintings.
3 They're building a <u>huge</u> new shopping centre not far from here.
4 The stadium is very <u>easy to get to</u> because it's near the station.
5 The weather was so <u>windy and wet</u> that we decided to stay at home.
6 When my mother met her sister again after two years, they were both very <u>deeply affected</u> when they saw each other.
7 There's a <u>strange and unusual</u> atmosphere in the mountains at night.
8 You kicked the football, so you are <u>to blame</u> for the broken window.
9 I quite enjoyed the film, but the ending was <u>not surprising</u>.

Listening Part 1

EXAM ADVICE

Read the questions first as they tell you what to listen for.

▶ 04 You hear people talking in eight different situations. For questions 1–8, choose the best answer (A, B or C).

1 You overhear someone talking to a tour guide. Why is she talking to him?
   A to make a complaint
   B to make a suggestion
   C to ask for advice

2 You hear a girl talking to a friend about a place she visited on holiday with her family. What did she like best about it?
   A the countryside
   B the entertainment
   C the shops

3 You overhear two people talking about a holiday. What went wrong?
   A The hotel was full.
   B The suitcases got lost.
   C The plane was delayed.

4 You hear a boy talking to his father on the phone. He asks his father to
   A meet him outside school.
   B pick him up later than agreed.
   C let him go to his friend Jim's house.

5 You hear two teenagers talking about a TV programme they saw. What do they agree about?
   A The filming was clever.
   B The presenter was lively.
   C The music was good.

6 You hear the following announcement on a train. What is the man doing?
   A warning about a cancellation
   B making a recommendation
   C confirming a change

7 You hear a brother and a sister talking about a car journey they are going on. What is the girl most concerned about?
   A the length of the journey
   B how bored they will be
   C taking enough food with them

8 You hear two teenagers talking about something that happened on a train journey. The girl feels
   A embarrassed.
   B relieved.
   C confused.

Reading and Use of English Part 3

For questions 1–8, read the text below. Use the word given in capitals at the end of some of the lines to form a word that fits the gap in the same line. There is an example at the beginning (0).

Our summer in Cornwall

Last year my family went to Cornwall, in the south west of Britain, for our summer holiday. My brother and I went surfing, but my parents, who aren't very (0) *adventurous*, spent their time reading and painting on the beach. They were able to do this every day because, (1) .... for Cornwall, it didn't rain at all while we were there. My mother's an artist, and she loves Cornwall because of its (2) .... beauty and the light, which she says is (3) ....

USUAL
NATURE
REMARK

My brother and I focused on developing our surfing skills. We were told which areas to avoid, because it was too (4) .... to surf there. The local people were very (5) ...., and told us which parts of the sea to treat with caution. They can also predict when and where dangerous currents will probably be. The most (6) .... day for me was when I (7) .... rode a huge wave, without falling off my board; it was absolutely (8) ....!

RISK
FRIEND
MEMORY
SUCCESS
THRILL

4 Food, glorious food

Grammar

so, such, too, enough, little, few

1 Complete the sentences. Choose A, B or C.
1. We have (A) *too many* (B) *enough* (C) *so few* milk.
2. I only eat (A) *too few* (B) *a little* (C) *too much* meat.
3. It was (A) *such a* (B) *so* (C) *such* delicious meal.
4. I've got (A) *so much* (B) *so many* (C) *so little* tomatoes in my garden this year.
5. There aren't (A) *too little* (B) *so few* (C) *enough* eggs to make a cake.
6. The recipe was (A) *too much* (B) *so* (C) *such* hard to understand.
7. There's (A) *few* (B) *little* (C) *such* time to cook in the evenings.
8. The market has (A) *such* (B) *few* (C) *so* fresh food.
9. This coffee is (A) *too* (B) *enough* (C) *so much* hot to drink.
10. I don't eat (A) *so much* (B) *few* (C) *enough* vegetables.

2 Some of these sentences contain mistakes. Correct the mistakes you find and put a tick (✓) next to the sentences which are correct.
1. I can't eat these potatoes. I don't think they were cooked for long enough. ......✓......
2. It only takes ~~so few~~ time to make an omelette.
   ......*a little*......
3. The problem is some people eat too little vegetables.
   ....
4. Most of the food we buy in supermarkets has too much packaging. ....
5. It's been such long time since I've had fresh strawberries. ....
6. This soup is much too cold to eat. Let's warm it up, shall we? ....
7. There's so many salt in this that I can't eat it.
   ....
8. The restaurant wasn't so good as I had expected.
   ....
9. He can cook much more better than I can. ....
10. There isn't enough tomatoes for the salad. ....

Vocabulary

Food and diet

1 EP Circle the correct word.
1. I generally prefer healthy *food* / *diet* like salads to things like hamburgers.
2. The dishes in this cookery book are very *elaborate* / *exclusive* and contain too many ingredients.
3. Athletes need to eat a very well-balanced *diet* / *food*.
4. Some people eat only raw *food* / *meals* because they think it's healthier.
5. You need to know how to cook a few *simple* / *fresh* dishes.
6. *Convenience* / *Organic* food often contains too much salt.
7. Don't eat *filling* / *heavy* snacks just before your main meal.
8. Experts have warned there may be a water *supply* / *shortage* this year.
9. Insects are becoming popular as a *food* / *diet* source.
10. We eat our main *meal* / *dish* at about 8 p.m.

2 EP Find the names of eight food-related words in the wordsearch. Use them to complete the sentences below.

H	B	A	N	A	N	S	J	F
S	M	A	N	P	P	P	U	A
E	P	R	O	T	E	I	N	D
A	D	L	E	L	O	N	K	A
W	H	E	R	B	S	A	A	I
E	R	A	F	E	A	C	N	R
E	Y	A	A	T	E	H	P	Y
D	E	T	T	A	R	G	A	E
S	C	A	N	T	E	E	N	S

1. Insects are a great source of ....
2. .... is a green vegetable which is often eaten raw in salads or in pasta dishes.
3. Milk and cheese are types of .... food.
4. .... is found growing on rocks in the ocean.
5. People should eat less .... food.
6. .... like mint are added to some dishes to improve the taste.
7. Chocolate isn't good for you because it contains sugar and ....
8. Students eat their meals at school in the ....

16

Writing Part 2 A review

Read some restaurant reviews written by students. Their teacher has made some comments. Match each comment with a review.

Teacher's comments
1 The information isn't given in a logical order.
  Review ....
2 The style is too informal.
  Review ....
3 The use of descriptive language is repetitive.
  Review ....
4 The grammatical range is very simple.
  Review ....
5 It includes irrelevant information.
  Review ....

Student reviews

A For dessert we had a really nice cheesecake. It was the nicest cheesecake I had ever tasted. It was even nicer than the cheesecake my grandmother makes and her cheesecake is very, very nice.

B It was my friend's 14th birthday so we ordered a big cake for her as a surprise. As soon as the waiter appeared with the cake, everyone in the restaurant started singing 'Happy Birthday'. My friend was really embarrassed.

C We complained about the service but the manager didn't seem bothered. I think that's terrible. I mean, if a customer complains, the manager should do something about it. My dad says he doesn't know how a restaurant like that can survive. The food's rubbish anyway; it's not just the service that's bad.

D I like Dylan's restaurant because the food is delicious. The waiters are really friendly and there is a good atmosphere there. All my friends like this restaurant because the food is good and it isn't expensive.

E It's an unusual place because everyone sits together at long tables, so you have to talk to people you have never met before. There's no menu, only a list of two or three dishes on a blackboard. This means the food is always really fresh. I like sitting with people I don't know because you meet some interesting people that way.

Reading and Use of English Part 4

EXAM ADVICE

Make sure you use the word given without changing it.

For questions 1–6, complete the second sentence so that it has a similar meaning to the first sentence, using the word given. **Do not change the word given.** You must use between **two** and **five** words, including the word given. Here is an example (0).

Example:

0 They only had a little money to spend at the supermarket.
  MUCH
  They ....*didn't have much*........ money to spend at the supermarket.

Write **only** the missing words **IN CAPITAL LETTERS**.

1 I'd rather eat at home than go out.
  INSTEAD
  I'd rather eat at home .... out.

2 'I suggest you have the fish,' the waiter said to me.
  ADVISED
  The waiter .... the fish.

3 There weren't enough eggs to make pancakes for breakfast.
  FEW
  There .... eggs to make pancakes for breakfast.

4 This dish needs more salt in it.
  ENOUGH
  This dish .... in it.

5 'I'm sorry, Madam, the fish has all gone.'
  LEFT
  'I'm sorry, Madam, there .... now.'

6 This chocolate cake recipe is better than the one my mother uses.
  AS
  The chocolate cake recipe my mother uses .... this one.

Unit 4

Listening Part 2

EXAM ADVICE

Before you listen, read the questions and think about the kind of word or words which might fit each gap.

▶ 05 You will hear an interview with Noah Beesdale, who is training to be a chef. For questions 1–10, complete the sentences with a word or short phrase.

RUNNING A RESTAURANT

Noah says the **(1)** .... of running a restaurant is enjoyable, although he realises it can be worrying too.

Noah thinks customers return to his uncle's restaurant because of the **(2)** .... it offers.

Noah says creating a good **(3)** .... is very important for developing a successful restaurant.

Noah has to identify the **(4)** .... before he makes one of his uncle's dishes.

Noah is pleased when he sees an excellent **(5)** .... of the restaurant.

There was a problem with the restaurant a few years ago because people only went there for a **(6)** ....

Noah says paying attention to **(7)** .... is how his uncle maintains a consistent level of service.

More than **(8)** .... people phone to book a table at the restaurant every day when the weather is good.

Noah likes the fact that cooking is **(9)** .... so the menu changes regularly.

In **(10)** .... they begin to cook richer food.

Reading and Use of English Part 3

For questions **1–8**, read the text below. Use the word given in capitals at the end of some of the lines to form a word that fits in the gap **in the same line**. There is an example at the beginning (**0**).

Edible rooftops

As you probably know, the cost of producing and distributing food is becoming
(0) ....*increasingly*.... expensive and prices are rising rapidly. In many cities   **INCREASE**
around the world this has led to a new (1) .... to produce food   **MOVE**
which is grown (2) .... The idea is to cut the distances food has **LOCAL**
to travel and to have (3) .... sources of fresh vegetables available **RELY**
for those of us who live in big cities.

The main (4) .... with growing vegetables in a city is that land is   **DIFFICULT**
very expensive, so using space which is being wasted at the moment, such as rooftops,
is seen as one (5) ....   **SOLVE**

Obviously it would be (6) .... for rooftop gardens to provide   **POSSIBLE**
all the vegetables needed for a whole city, especially as rooftops are not the
(7) .... places to grow vegetables. Plants need a good supply of   **EASY**
rainwater and some (8) .... from the wind. Do you think it could   **PROTECT**
work where you live?

5 Study time

Grammar

Zero, first and second conditionals

Complete each sentence with the correct tense of the verb in brackets.

1. I ......*would enjoy*...... (enjoy) shopping if I could buy anything I wanted.
2. You wouldn't catch cold all the time if you .... (wear) warmer clothes.
3. We'll never finish getting the room ready unless everyone .... (help).
4. Your teacher will be annoyed if you .... (not make) more effort to hand in your homework on time.
5. If we .... (want) to improve our football team's performance, we will have to train harder.
6. Don't miss any lessons unless you .... (be) ill.
7. If I .... (have) more money, I would buy a better skateboard.
8. Please contact me if you .... (need) to ask any questions.
9. If I were allowed to, I .... (come) to the concert.
10. If you carry on straight ahead, you .... (see) the sports centre on the right.

Vocabulary

Words often confused

1. These sentences contain incorrect words. Use the words in the box below to help you correct them.

   attend (x2)   expect   find out   get to know
   join   see   ~~teach~~

   1. I've ~~learned~~ lots of children how to swim. ......*taught*......
   2. Your train doesn't arrive till 7.45 so I'll attend you to arrive here at about eight. ....
   3. I assist the same school as my brother. ....
   4. Every student was given a questionnaire to know what their likes and dislikes were. ....
   5. Membership of the sports club didn't cost much so I decided to take part in it. ....
   6. There is a party on the first night of the course so students can know each other. ....
   7. One hundred guests took part in the wedding. ....
   8. We bought two tickets to attend the new film. ....

Phrasal verbs

2. **EP** Replace each underlined word or phrase with a phrasal verb from the box. Put it in the correct tense.

   find out   get through   get away with   ~~look back~~
   point out   put off   sort out   turn out

   When I (1) <u>think about the past</u> ......*look back*...... , one of the happiest periods of my life was between the ages of 5 and 11 when we lived on a tiny island. There were about six children on the island and we were taught by our parents. We spent a lot of time playing on the beach and in the fields as our parents thought that was a good way to (2) <u>learn</u> .... about life. They (3) <u>told us about</u> .... any activities that were really dangerous, but most of the time we (4) <u>weren't punished for</u> .... doing all kinds of naughty things and we had to (5) <u>solve</u> .... any problems or arguments ourselves. Of course, we all preferred being outside to studying and (6) <u>delayed</u> .... doing our homework as long as we could. Despite this, we (7) <u>succeeded in</u> .... our primary-level tests and it all (8) <u>ended</u> .... well as we are all at secondary school now.

Study words

3 **EP** Read this conversation between a teacher and a pupil. Find the missing words in the wordsearch. Look in all directions.

Teacher: Is your brother studying psychology at university now, Adam?
Adam: Yes, it's quite hard. In fact, he didn't think he'd get through the (1) ...*admission*... process because there's so much competition for the (2) .... he chose.
Teacher: Well, he did well in his end-of-school exams so he deserved to get a place.
Adam: He got good (3) .... in most subjects but his best results weren't in (4) .... subjects. He's always done really well at art and technology. I know he sometimes wonders if he's made the right choice.
Teacher: Well, he'll have a (5) .... in psychology at the end. I'm sure the job (6) .... are very good – there are lots of things he could do afterwards.
Adam: Yeah, that's true. He told me he's finding some of the (7) .... quite challenging. He's spending loads of time doing the (8) .... for it.
Teacher: Doesn't he have a (9) .... who can help?
Adam: He does, and he sees him at (10) .... a couple of times a week. He says he's not always sure what to ask, though.
Teacher: I'm sure he'll be fine. Give him my best wishes when you see him!
Adam: Thanks, I will.

C	L	T	T	F	E	F	U	E	T	N
W	O	E	O	E	L	R	E	G	U	H
N	D	U	R	O	T	U	T	S	T	J
E	E	G	R	T	E	A	N	U	O	A
P	E	S	U	S	A	E	R	E	R	C
D	E	T	E	D	E	O	C	O	I	A
M	A	R	K	S	A	W	A	H	A	D
C	O	U	R	S	E	D	O	A	L	E
R	E	S	E	A	R	C	H	R	S	M
P	R	O	S	P	E	C	T	S	K	I
N	O	I	S	S	I	M	D	A	C	C

Word formation – suffixes

4 **EP** Use the following suffixes to change the verbs in the box into nouns: *-ation, -ence, -ment* or *-ance*. Write them in the correct column.

~~admire~~   amaze   appear   apply   arrange   assist   concentrate   encourage   exist   differ   guide   identify   perform   prefer   publish   punish

-ation	-ence	-ment	-ance
admiration			

5 Complete these sentences with appropriate nouns from the table.

1 My mother was very excited about the .... of her first novel.
2 Having a bicycle would make a huge .... to my life.
3 To my .... , I won a prize for the song I wrote.
4 People didn't know of the .... of the planet Uranus until Hirschel discovered it in 1871.
5 Staff are available to offer .... to anyone who needs help carrying their luggage.

Unit 5

Reading and Use of English Part 6

You are going to read an article for American teenagers going to summer camp to study or to do other activities. Six sentences have been removed from the article. Choose from the sentences **A–G** the one which fits each gap (**1–6**). There is one extra sentence which you do not need to use.

EXAM ADVICE

When you have chosen a sentence for each gap, read the text before and after the gap again to check your answers.

Going to a Summer Sleepaway Camp

Going to sleepaway camp is a summertime tradition for many kids in the United States. It's called sleepaway camp because you stay overnight there. Kids typically stay at sleepaway camp for a week or longer. You might go to a camp where you can swim, do crafts, or work on your sports skills. You could also go to a camp where you study something, like computers, outer space, or literature.

No matter which kind of sleepaway camp you're going to, you're probably excited – and maybe a little nervous if it's your first time. Be proud of yourself for being grown-up enough to go to camp. It might be a chance to try new things, or to learn more about a subject you're interested in. **1** It's also an opportunity to learn a little more about being independent.

Many kids go to day camps during the summer. **2** You start camp in the morning and go home in the afternoon. Like anything, it might take you a little while to get adjusted to the place, the camp counselors, and the kids. But you come home every night, just like you do during the school year.

Sleepaway camp offers some additional excitement because you'll be at the camp all day and night. **3** This makes it into a kind of vacation, but without your parents. You'll probably sleep in a cabin or dorm with other kids attending the camp. You'll probably eat together in a large cafeteria.

Usually, the camp mails out information to your family before you go, so you'll know what to bring. Just like any vacation, you'll need to pack a bag (or two) full of the clothes and other stuff you'll need while you're there. Food is generally provided. **4** Camp counselors (who are usually grown-ups and older teens) will be on hand to lead activities and look after you. For instance, if you scrape your knee, a camp counselor can help you get it cleaned up and bandaged. But best of all, camp counselors help kids have fun at camp. They and other grown-ups at camp are responsible for taking care of you, but campers can do a lot to take care of themselves. **5** You'll want to take it seriously when a counselor tells you not to wander away from the group if you're on a hike in the woods.

With so much to do, it's tough to be bored at camp. But you might find that you feel a little homesick. Homesickness is the feeling of missing your everyday familiar life, like your parents, your room, and maybe even your brother or sister. **6** You might be able to call home to talk with your family. You could also email or write letters to your family and friends. If you're feeling down, it can help to talk with other campers or your counselors about your feelings. But it's also OK if you **don't** feel lonely because you're too busy enjoying yourself. That's the idea, after all.

A There are things you can do about it, though.
B They can be a lot of fun too, but the schedule is familiar.
C However, camp is even more than just making friends and having fun, or studying something you enjoy.
D So, of course, that means having your meals there and sleeping over.
E That's why it might be worth finding out how the camp organises them before you leave home.
F Even so, it might be a good idea to take some extra money for snacks or other small expenses.
G This means following the safety rules when it comes to doing things such as swimming and boating.

Listening Part 3

▶06 You will hear five short extracts in which British teenagers are talking about why they like a particular school subject best. For questions 1–5, choose from the list (A–H) the reason each speaker gives. Use the letters only once. There are three extra letters which you do not need to use.

A I can talk to my parents about it.
B I can sit with my friends in class.
C I find it easy.
D I don't have to do much homework for it.
E I like the textbook.
F I think it will be useful for me in the future.
G I have an excellent teacher.
H I enjoy the challenge of it.

Speaker 1 [1]
Speaker 2 [2]
Speaker 3 [3]
Speaker 4 [4]
Speaker 5 [5]

Reading and Use of English Part 3

For questions 1–8, read the text below. Use the word given in capitals at the end of some of the lines to form a word that fits in the gap **in the same line**. There is an example at the beginning (0).

EXAM ADVICE

Check you have spelt your answers correctly.

Stay with a family abroad!

We (0) ...... *originally* ...... founded our organisation to give English teenagers   ORIGIN
the opportunity to go and stay with French families to learn the language. Then
we realised that it made sense to run an exchange programme, and expanded to
include several different countries.

Having the chance to practise a language in the country in which it is spoken is, of
course, very (1) .... and really helps the learning process. Going on   EFFECT
an exchange allows learners to mix with local (2) .... and in this way   INHABIT
they can acquire a greater and deeper (3) .... of the people whose   KNOW
language they are studying.

If you think you'd be interested in participating in our exchange programme, why not
contact us to discuss your particular (4) .... ? From the information   REQUIRE
you give us, we can make some (5) .... and suggest several different   RECOMMEND
(6) .... We want to avoid you going somewhere   POSSIBLE
(7) .... and not making the most of the experience. Our aim is that all   SUIT
our students have a truly (8) .... time.   MEMORY

My first job

Grammar
Articles

1 Complete each gap with *a*, *the* or *–*.

Working in films

You don't need to be (1) ....*a*.... famous actor to get (2) .... part on (3) .... film set but you need to be willing to start at (4) .... bottom. For example, you could spend hours standing in (5) .... rain by (6) .... gate in (7) .... field stopping (8) .... people from coming in.
In (9) .... Britain and most other countries, you should look for (10) .... job as (11) .... 'runner'. Runners fetch things and help generally. This is (12) .... most junior job and even if you want to be (13) .... camera operator, it's (14) .... good place to start. You could do (15) .... training course but (16) .... best qualification is (17) .... experience.

Countable and uncountable nouns

2 Complete each sentence with a word from the box. You don't need to use all the words but you will need to make some of them plural.

> advice dish equipment experience food
> information knowledge luggage ~~meal~~
> scenery suggestion suitcase tool view

1 There are few ....*meals*.... of two courses which can be prepared in less than 20 minutes.
2 If you take up climbing you will need to buy .... like a helmet and boots.
3 The amount of .... the average family eats in Britain seems to go up every year.
4 My family always travels with a large number of .... so we all have to carry something.
5 Jack sends long emails but they contain little .... about what he's doing.
6 We climbed to the top of the tower where the .... were spectacular.
7 Here are a few .... on how to get a Saturday job in a café.
8 My mum cooks a traditional .... like beetroot soup every weekend.
9 My parents always take a bus to the station when we go on holiday unless we have a great deal of ....
10 My sister got a job in a shop even though she had little .... in advertising.

Vocabulary
Adjective collocations with *job* and *work*

1 **EP** For each sentence, choose a word from the box. Then circle *job* or *work* in each sentence.

> weekend   outdoor   paid   skilled
> full-time   temporary

1 My dad has a .... job / work – he works eight hours a day, five days a week.
2 My sister can't afford to live on what she earns – she needs to find a well-.............. job / work.
3 My brother's looking for .... job / work – he doesn't mind what it is but he's only free on Saturdays and Sundays.
4 My cousin's only working there for six weeks because it's a .... job / work.
5 You need qualifications and training to be a mechanic – it's .... job / work.
6 .... job / work can be very demanding in the winter but my dad prefers it to working in an office.

24

Words often confused

2 👁 Five of the sentences below contain an incorrect word. Correct them and put a tick (✓) next to the sentences which are correct.

1 I saw a really funny programme on TV last night. ....✓........
2 My cousin's not working tomorrow so he'll take the ~~possibility~~ to play tennis. ....*opportunity*....
3 Thirty years ago, people didn't have so many occasions to travel. ....
4 My father's written a novel and there's an opportunity it might be published. ....
5 The gymnastics course will be funny as the other teenagers on it are friendly. ....
6 I'll lend you my necklace as it's a special occasion. ....
7 Is there a possibility that you could come round on Saturday instead of Friday? ....
8 My sister's been offered a wonderful occasion to play at a music festival. ....

Writing Part 2 · A letter

1 Read the exam question below. Then complete each gap in the reply with a linking word or phrase from the box.

> You have received a letter from an American student called Jay. Read this part of the letter and then write your letter to Jay.
>
> During the summer holidays, I'm going to get a part-time job. Do people do this in your country and what sort of jobs do people do?
> Write soon,
> Jay
>
> Write your letter in 140–190 words in an appropriate style.

although	both	~~but~~	for the same reason,
if you like,	so	as a result	
the disadvantage is that	on the other hand,		

My first job

Dear Jay, Thank you for your letter. I have a job in a shop near where I live. I work every Saturday (1) ......*but*...... in the holidays I work three days a week. (2) .... I enjoy the contact with people, it's a shoe shop and I'm not really interested in what I'm selling! Most people don't want to work in the evening (3) .... it's not too difficult to get an evening or weekend job in a supermarket. Some even stay open all night! (4) .... school kids and students often work in restaurants and cafés because that's usually evening and weekend work too so people often get jobs as waiters. (5) .... during term time, it can be hard to get all your homework done as well. (6) .... it's great to have a bit of money to spend, especially during the holidays! (7) .... the jobs I've mentioned are hard work. However, that tends to be the kind of part-time work available for teenagers in my area. (8) .... I'll send you some pictures of me in the shoe shop – then you'll be able to see what sort of place I work in! I hope you find a job you enjoy. Best wishes, Ben

2 Answer these questions.
1 Which jobs does Ben write about?
2 What explanation does he give for why teenagers do these jobs?
3 Which job does he suggest is best? What reasons does he give?

3 The letter doesn't have any paragraphs. Mark where they should go.

Unit 6

Listening Part 1

▶07 You will hear people talking in eight different situations. For questions 1–8, choose the best answer (A, B or C).

1. You overhear two teenagers talking. Where are they?
   A in a shop
   B in a café
   C at home

2. You hear a teenager talking on the phone about a part-time job he has been offered. How does he feel?
   A confused
   B upset
   C disappointed

3. You hear a girl talking to her teacher about her holiday job. She says it's
   A tiring.
   B interesting.
   C exciting.

4. You hear a woman talking to a group of teenagers. What is she doing?
   A asking for information
   B giving advice
   C explaining a decision

5. You hear two teenagers talking about babysitting. What do they agree about?
   A It's fun.
   B It's well paid.
   C It's an easy job.

6. You hear a teenager talking to his boss. What excuse does he give for being late?
   A He didn't have any transport.
   B He wasn't given information he needed.
   C He had to help someone.

7. You hear a message on a telephone answering service. The speaker wants to
   A offer thanks.
   B make a suggestion.
   C change a plan.

8. You hear a girl talking to a friend. What job does she prefer?
   A waitress
   B kitchen assistant
   C receptionist

Reading and Use of English Part 7

You are going to read an article about being a newspaper reporter. For questions 1–10, choose from the people (A–_). The people may be chosen more than once.

Which person says

they had a particular advantage when applying for one job?	1 ☐
time for research is often limited?	2 ☐
their present job is good training for their future career?	3 ☐
they find it difficult when they are not permitted to finish something?	4 ☐
it is important to take advantage of subject areas you know a lot about?	5 ☐
a wide range of general knowledge is important?	6 ☐
it is important not to make mistakes?	7 ☐
they may not advance steadily in their career?	8 ☐
it is important for them to build links with the community?	9 ☐
that journalists should not let their own point of view influence what they write?	10 ☐

Working in the news

My first job

Newspaper journalists or reporters source, research and write stories for publication in local, regional and national press. Four young reporters tell us what it's like for them and offer tips for those who are hoping to become journalists.

A Craig

As a reporter, you really have to be ready for anything. A story could come up on a subject you know nothing about and you may have just half an hour to read a report or past stories before you interview someone. I spend most of my time in the office, unfortunately. My advice for potential journalists is that you need to be able to speak to anyone in all walks of life. A story could come up where the subject is close to your heart but you have to be unbiased and open to other people's opinions, even if you do not agree with them. Every subject is useful – you need to know a little bit about everything.

B Beth

I would say about 60% of my time is spent inside the office. The experienced journalists usually visit people in their houses as it makes for a much better story, and sometimes I get to go with them, but unfortunately this is not always possible. The unpaid work experience I'm doing during the holidays at a local newspaper will be a great advantage when I apply for a job after I leave school. They may not seem that important, but local newspapers are a great source of news for national newspapers. The general agreement at my newspaper is that the story can be passed on as long as it has appeared in our paper or on our website first. To be a journalist you must be outgoing and professional, and you also have to ensure accuracy in all stories. You have to be able to talk to all sorts of people.

C Andrew

My dad's first job was with a regional paper, and I'm doing something similar. I think the editor was impressed by the fact that I come from the area and know about local issues. I'd like to end up working from home on a freelance basis, maybe writing features for the Sunday newspapers. You have to be very self-motivated and able to generate ideas for new stories all the time. I know from seeing what happened to my dad that journalism isn't a profession where you progress upwards from one position to the next. I know that's probably going to be my experience, too. You need to be prepared to work hard to get work experience, get a qualification and demonstrate your commitment. My dad always says that if you're a specialist in anything (sport, music, computer games), you should write about it, and I'm sure he's right.

D Deborah

I had no career plan at all when I graduated – I found work with a very small, family-owned paper where I found myself doing all sorts of jobs. While there I decided to train as a journalist. I must be the only person in the universe to 'fall into' journalism! A crucial part of my job is building contacts locally. I attend a lot of council meetings to try to find out what is going on with the 15,000 employees and attend numerous other meetings. Why do I do it? It's certainly not for the money, which is very poor. I really enjoy seeing my words change things. The frustrations include leaving a story I'm enjoying working on because the editor wants something else.

High adventure

Grammar

Infinitive and verb + -ing

1 Complete the sentences with the correct form of the verb in brackets (the infinitive or -ing form). In some of the sentences, both are correct.

1. I began .... (go) snowboarding when I was five years old.
2. There was no point .... (try) to windsurf yesterday because there wasn't enough wind.
3. We continued .... (train) for the race even though the weather was terrible.
4. I stopped .... (rest) after running for five kilometres.
5. Remember, as it's closed, ... (not go) to school tomorrow.
6. I started .... (do) rock climbing when I was a university student.
7. Don't forget .... (bring) plenty of water on the climbing trip.
8. It wasn't worth .... (continue) up the mountain because we couldn't see anything through the mist.
9. My family stopped .... (visit) Scotland every summer when my grandparents moved.
10. I prefer .... (sail) on the sea to on a lake.
11. I was offered a place in the regional swimming team but it meant .... (travel) to competitions every weekend.
12. I meant .... (tell) Oliver about my new part-time job when I saw him but I forgot.

2 Complete the sentences with a verb from the box that both fits grammatically and makes sense. There are two verbs which you don't need to use.

admitted	allowed	avoided	decided
expected	failed	promised	succeeded
thought	warned

1. My parents weren't happy about it but they .... me to go paragliding when I was 14.
2. My father only .... to learn how to snowboard when he was 50 and now he's better than me!
3. Everyone .... Daniel to win the race so they were surprised when he lost.
4. The ski instructor .... taking us on the higher slopes because it was our first lesson.
5. The guide was really embarrassed when he .... not knowing the way home.
6. Unfortunately we .... to reach the top of the mountain because of the bad weather.
7. Nobody had .... about bringing a map in case we got lost.
8. The team were so happy when they .... in winning the silver cup.

Vocabulary

Phrasal verbs and expressions with *take*

1 EP Complete the sentences using the correct form of one of the expressions.

| take turns | take part in | take a risk | take exercise |
| take up to | take someone's place |

1. Everybody is welcome to .... the race.
2. Jack was injured so Andy .... on the team and played in the final instead.
3. A professional tennis match can .... five hours to complete.
4. If you don't .... when you're young, your health may suffer when you're older.
5. We decided to .... and go sailing even though the wind was quite strong.
6. There weren't enough tennis rackets for everyone so we had to .... playing.

2 Look at the phrasal verbs and their definitions. Then complete the sentences with the correct verb.

take sthg up	to start a new hobby or activity
take to sthg	to be good at, or enjoy something new
take after	to be similar to a member of your family
take off	to be a success, become established
take sthg on	to accept new challenges or responsibilities
take away	to remove

1 I take .... my father. He is scared of heights too.
2 I've been asked to take .... the role of captain of the hockey team next year.
3 My aunt's career as an underwater photographer has really taken .... Her photos are always in different magazines.
4 I think he should take .... a new challenge. Something like cross-country running would be good.
5 The injured rugby player was taken .... by ambulance.
6 I didn't think I'd enjoy it much but I really took .... snowboarding. It wasn't as difficult as I'd expected.

Verb collocations with sporting activities

3 Circle the correct word.

1 I didn't realise so many people were *watching / looking* me when my windsurf crashed into a boat.
2 People who enjoy *playing / doing* judo must be so fit.
3 What kind of sports do you enjoy *playing / doing*?
4 The crowd was cheering so loudly I couldn't *listen / hear* a word the referee was saying.
5 Shall we *watch / see* the football match you recorded this evening?
6 Alisha has been *doing / going* climbing every weekend for the last three months.

Writing Part 2 — A review

Find ten spelling mistakes in this review.

Review of our school trip to Brookwood Adventure Centre

Our class recently went on a school trip to Brookwood Adventure Centre. Brookwood is conviniently situated not too far away from the school near Bluewater Lake. It only took us two hours to get there by bus. There were twenty of us and we spent five days there on a sailing corse.

The acommodation was very confortable and spacious. The food was excelent, although some students said there wasn't enough choice. There are also cheap restaurants a short bycicle ride away.

The activities were well organised and safety standards were high. Students said they enjoyed the course despite the bad wether. Some students thought there weren't enough oportunities to practise sailing but they were impressed with the instructors, who were all extremely experienced. Each student was given a lot of personal attention, wich helped them to develop their confidence.

I belive this course was beneficial for all the participants. It was also good value for money. For these reasons I would recommend the course to other students our age, and I think the school should organise a similar trip next year.

High adventure

Unit 7

Listening Part 2

▶08 You will hear part of a radio interview with Barry Helman, a cave-diving expert. For questions 1–10, complete the sentences with a word or short phrase.

CAVE DIVING

Barry says it is the incredible beauty and (1) .... of the caves that attracts him to diving.

Barry compares himself to an (2) ....

Other divers say the danger is a (3) ....

Barry says the most frightening thing about cave diving is the complete (4) ....

Because it's not possible to get to the surface easily, having good (5) .... skills is essential for survival.

Most accidents involve people who take (6) .... when diving.

Not having enough (7) .... is a potentially dangerous problem.

You need to have proper (8) .... to do cave diving.

A good cave diver should never (9) .... when facing a serious problem.

Barry thinks being a good diver increases your (10) .... in normal life.

Reading and Use of English Part 2

EXAM ADVICE

Read the whole text when you have finished to make sure the words you have written make sense.

For questions 1–8, read the text below and think of the word which best fits each gap. Use only **one** word in each gap. There is an example at the beginning (0).

What is ski touring?

Ski touring is exactly that – touring on skis. It combines (0) ....*the*.... best bits of skiing and mountaineering and provides the perfect way to explore the mountains in winter. The advantages (1) .... ski touring are that you can really escape the crowds, enjoy the solitude of the mountains and (2) .... rewarded with breathtaking views and exhilarating descents.

Ski touring involves both going up and down the mountain, so even for experienced skiers new skills (3) .... to be acquired. (4) .... is much to learn about 'skinning up' (getting up the mountain) that improves efficiency and saves energy. Similarly, you want to be (5) .... to enjoy going down, which means learning to cope with the variety of snow conditions you will encounter off-piste. (6) .... all ski touring is very demanding, you must be (7) .... good physical condition. The fitter you are, the (8) .... fun you will have.

High adventure

Reading and Use of English Part 1

For questions 1–8, read the text below and decide which answer (A, B, C or D) best fits each gap. There is an example at the beginning (0).

EXAM ADVICE

Some questions test words which are part of fixed expressions.

Example:

0 **A** make   **B** do   **C** ensure   **D** have

Planning a day out for your class

Researching your destination properly will **(0)** .... all aspects of your class trip easier, as well as helping you to **(1)** .... the most out of the experience. You'll be in a better position to pick the best places to go and you'll also learn what you need to take with you, as well as any potential difficulties you should be **(2)** .... of, for example there may be steep hills to climb and everybody will need comfortable shoes.

The season and ticket prices are important **(3)** .... in your decision about when to go. If you're going to be outdoors, bad weather or weather you're not **(4)** .... for can ruin the trip. While you can't predict what the **(5)** .... weather will be, make sure you always check the forecast in advance.

While some research is absolutely **(6)** .... , don't plan every moment of your day in advance. Over-planning tends to make people less **(7)** .... to take part in the surprising and spontaneous **(8)** .... that are potentially part of any sort of trip. Above all, the aim of the day is for everyone to enjoy themselves as much as possible.

1 A take	B get	C find	D set
2 A aware	B familiar	C informed	D knowledgeable
3 A points	B reasons	C factors	D details
4 A anticipated	B prepared	C expected	D planned
5 A accurate	B correct	C true	D exact
6 A needed	B essential	C ideal	D useful
7 A curious	B interested	C attracted	D willing
8 A circumstances	B performances	C events	D chances

8 Dream of the stars

Grammar
Reported speech

1 Anita asked her friends what they thought about a television programme and wrote down what they told her. Write the words each person actually said.

Anita's speech bubble: For my English homework, I want to write about a television programme called *Life swap*. What do you think about it?

Anita

1 Lucy told me she would definitely watch the whole series.
2 Jessica said her whole family had watched it the day before and they had all liked it.
3 Harry said he had never seen it and he didn't want to.
4 Grace said she was going to watch it the following week.
5 Daniel told me he couldn't wait for the next episode because he was really enjoying it.
6 Charlie said he had only seen one episode and it had been a bit boring but he might watch it again.

1 Lucy: *I'll definitely watch the whole series.*
2 Jessica: ....
....
3 Harry: ....
....
4 Grace: ....
....
5 Daniel: ....
....
6 Charlie: ....
....

Reporting verbs

2 Match what the people said (A–G) with a reporting verb from the box.

> admit   announce   complain   ~~inform~~
> promise   recommend   warn

A The bus leaves at two thirty.
   inform

B The city centre can be dangerous at night.
   ....

C This food tastes disgusting.
   ....

D I will give the money back tomorrow.
   ....

E I'm going to live in Brazil.
   ....

F I told a lie.
   ....

G You should watch the new James Bond film.
   ....

3 Now report what the people in Exercise 2 said.

1 The bus driver informed us that
   the bus left at two thirty.
2 Filip complained that
   ....
3 Beatriz promised that
   ....
4 Paul announced that
   ....
5 Karima recommended that
   ....
6 Roberto warned that
   ....
7 Tereza admitted that
   ....

Vocabulary

Entertainment

1 **EP** Read the clues and complete the crossword.

Across
1. The .... was first performed in this theatre in 1934.
2. This entrance is for actors only whereas the other entrance is for the general ....
3. I'm a TV .... so I have to make all the practical arrangements for a programme.
4. The first .... on last night's quiz show won £10,000.
5. My favourite actor was only in the first .... of the play unfortunately.
7. A law was passed to give famous people greater .... from the press.
10. The two singers sang together on .... for the first time in 20 years.
12. The .... started clapping as soon as the band were announced.
13. The film was made on .... in Hawaii.
14. The .... was excellent, despite none of the actors being professional.
15. The second episode in the new .... about musicians was much better than the first.

Down
1. At the beginning of the show, the .... told everyone what the prizes were.
2. The main actor's .... wasn't as good as usual tonight.
6. This magazine always has an article about the life of a famous ....
8. Most Bollywood films are made in film .... in Mumbai.
9. There were more .... than usual at the football match.
11. A .... is a newspaper which has short reports and a lot of photos.

Verb collocations with *ambition*, *career*, *experience* and *job*

2 **EP** Choose the correct word, A–D, for each gap.

1. Anna had a real talent for dance and eventually ......*fulfilled*...... her ambition to dance at the Lincoln Center in New York.
   A fulfilled   **B** concluded   **C** succeeded   **D** convinced

2. If you .... work experience and want to help the environment, you could offer to do voluntary conservation work.
   A miss   **B** abandon   **C** lack   **D** deny

3. Gerry is determined to .... a career with animals and his dream is to set up his own practice as a vet.
   A launch   **B** pursue   **C** realise   **D** perform

4. If you want to .... experience of working with children, you could do some babysitting for your cousins.
   A get   **B** achieve   **C** earn   **D** make

5. I turned .... a Saturday job in a supermarket because I'd rather work in an amusement park if I can.
   A up   **B** out   **C** back   **D** down

Unit 8

Listening Part 3

▶09 You will hear five short extracts in which people are talking about a film they have seen. For questions 1–5, choose from the list (A–H) what each person thinks about the film. Use the letters only once. There are three extra letters which you do not need to use.

A It was boring.
B It was too brief.
C It was set in the wrong location.
D The action scenes were unconvincing.
E The plot was too complicated.
F It was too serious.
G One of the actors let the others down.
H The acting was poor.

Speaker 1 [1]
Speaker 2 [2]
Speaker 3 [3]
Speaker 4 [4]
Speaker 5 [5]

Reading and Use of English Part 4

For questions 1–6, complete the second sentence so it has a similar meaning to the first sentence, using the word given. **Do not change the word given.** You must use between **two** and **five** words, including the word given. Here is an example (0).

Example:

0 The train driver said, 'The train will be 30 minutes late.'
   DELAY
   The train driver announced that there ....*would be a delay*....... of 30 minutes.

1 I had an invitation from Miranda to join her ice skating tomorrow.
   GO
   Miranda invited .... ice skating with her and her friends the next day.

2 Lee told me he was sorry that he hadn't come to my party.
   FOR
   Lee apologised .... to my party.

3 Alice told Tom she thought he had scratched her phone.
   OF
   Alice accused .... her phone.

4 In the end I got my sister to agree that I could borrow her dress.
   LEND
   I finally persuaded .... her dress.

5 My dad told the hotel receptionist that our room was too small.
   ABOUT
   My dad complained .... too small to the hotel receptionist.

6 She was warned by the policeman about the traffic jam ahead.
   THERE
   The policeman warned .... a traffic jam ahead.

Reading and Use of English Part 6

You are going to read an article about a teenage singer called Austin Mahone. Six sentences have been removed from the article. Choose from the sentences **A–G** the one which fills each gap (**1–6**). There is one extra sentence which you do not need to use.

'Teens can make it all happen', says pop star Austin Mahone

'I would say, no matter what people tell you, anything can happen.' That's the message internet singing sensation Austin Mahone says he'll deliver to 20,000 peers in the audience at *We Day* – an event for young people in Canada – and to tens of thousands watching the live stream of the event online.

But when the 17-year-old appears on stage, it won't even be necessary for him to sing or say anything in order to deliver his message. Quite simply, Austin has changed the way the world perceives him. **1** He's done it using social media.

When he was 14, Austin and a friend began uploading covers of pop-star songs to music websites. 'I was just doing it because me and my best friend were bored.' **2**

'I'd check different websites for the most popular songs, and I'd record my own versions,' he explains. 'That's how people began to find me online.' His videos got millions of hits and he signed with a record label. The result was Austin's debut, full-length, solo album, *Junior Year*. **3** He says he was sometimes criticised by his peers for posting his videos online. Yet this didn't put him off. 'I kept working hard. I was passionate about it.' And the hits on his videos kept coming. Austin eventually dropped out of school to focus on his career and opted for home schooling to finish his high-school education.

His passion, his perseverance and his achievement all make him a perfect fit for the message of *We Day*. After all, the aim of *Free The Children*, the international charity and creator of the event, is 'to empower and enable youth to be agents of change.' **4** It is well aware that young people don't tend to watch TV to find out what's going on in the world, they check online.

The fact that Austin has four million followers on a social networking site who will learn about the charity when he writes about his *We Day* appearance is an important contribution he can make, in addition to his presence at the event. Moreover, he's a hot commodity as an entertainer for exactly the demographic that attends *We Day*, and is planning to perform a hit single. The charity is certainly benefiting from his participation. **5** That's because Austin gets to reinforce his image as someone who volunteers his time and talent for a worthy cause and show that he cares about making the world a better place. **6** These were recently informed online that he had finally got his driving licence. Asked how he came to connect with the charity, Austin explains, 'My manager told me about it. They made a couple of calls.' He's looking forward to *We Day*, he says, because, 'I like to try new things, to travel. I get to perform, to meet new people.' His goal for the future: 'Hopefully win a couple of Grammy awards and go on a world tour.'

A Even Austin's remarkable rise by way of social media fits with the way the organisation operates and raises funds.

B He'll also have something meaningful to tell to his fans.

C He's living proof that every teen out there can, as he says, make anything happen.

D He knows that was the best way to deal with the publicity he'd been getting.

E While it seems like a meteoric rise for the teenager, Austin admits the early days were not always fun.

F His home town, he notes, didn't even have a bowling alley or a movie theatre.

G However, it's a win-win situation all round.

9 Secrets of the mind

Grammar

Modal verbs to express certainty and possibility

1 Rewrite the sentences in *italics* using a modal verb: *might, may, could, must* or *can't*.

1 Ryan is looking well. *I'm sure he's enjoying his holiday.*
   He ......*must be*...... enjoying his holiday.

2 Deborah seems a bit tired. *Perhaps she's working too hard.*
   She ....

3 He never comes skateboarding with us now. *I don't suppose he likes it any more.*
   He ....

4 She has a part-time job in a restaurant. *I imagine that's quite good fun.*
   That ....

5 That girl looks about ten. *She's definitely not Claire's little sister.*
   That ....

6 He's just bought two new computer games. *He obviously got some money for his birthday.*
   He ....

7 Andy and his brother aren't speaking to each other. *I don't believe they've had another argument.*
   They .... another argument.

8 You seem very familiar. *Perhaps we've met before.*
   We ....

9 My maths teacher says she doesn't speak English. *I'm sure she didn't learn it at school.*
   She .... at school.

10 I don't know why she didn't tell her dad she'd lost her phone. *It's possible she thought he would be angry.*
   She ....

2 Read the paragraph about risk-taking. Circle the correct modal verbs.

Psychologists believe that taking risks has always been part of human nature. For early humans, risk-taking (1) *must / can't* have been part of everyday life. Psychologists think that early human risk-takers (2) *may / can't* have been more likely to explore new places, possibly finding a new source of water or food. Such individuals (3) *can't / might* also have risked doing things differently, such as using a new kind of weapon or animal trap. These acts (4) *must / mustn't* have given the risk-taker a great sense of achievement, but (5) *can't / could* also have profoundly benefited his or her group by improving their lives in some way.

Writing Part 2 An article

You see this advertisement in your college magazine.

Articles wanted
Who has inspired you most?
A friend?   A family member?   Someone famous?
Tell us why you admire them and describe the influence this person has had on you.
The best article will appear in next term's magazine.

Write your article in 140–190 words.

1 Read the following introductory paragraphs.
1 Which title do you think has the most impact?
2 Which paragraph is about the right length?
3 Underline all the adjectives which describe personality and feelings.
4 Which paragraph repeats the same vocabulary and structures too often?

A
A living example
My favourite aunt has had a very big influence on me. She is my father's oldest sister and I spent a lot of time with her when I was growing up. She didn't have any children of her own so she treated all her nephews and nieces as if they were her own children. She was quite old-fashioned in many ways and could be quite critical if she didn't approve of our behaviour or our clothes. But at the same time she was always ready to listen to us and discuss our feelings without getting shocked or angry.

B
My favourite cousin
My family have all influenced me in different ways. My parents taught me to be responsible and to work hard. My grandmother taught me how to cook. But the person who has had the biggest impact on me is my cousin Robert because he taught me how to have fun and how to enjoy life.

2 Read the rest of *My favourite cousin*.
1 Find more adjectives that describe personality and feelings.
2 Replace the word *very* with a word from the box to add variety and interest. Can you use the modifying adverbs in the box in all the examples?

> extremely   particularly   really   quite

Robert was **(1)** *very* confident whereas I used to be **(2)** *very* shy and always stressed. But Robert taught me that being stressed doesn't help solve problems. Robert never got upset when things went wrong and I decided I wanted to be like him. So I stopped worrying so much and soon I began to enjoy life more.

A cousin who is a few years older can have a **(3)** *very* big influence. In my case Robert had a bigger influence than my older brother because that relationship was always **(4)** *very* competitive and my brother never wanted to spend time with me.

Now Robert and I have **(5)** *very* different jobs and interests but I will always be **(6)** *very* grateful to him for showing me that it's easy to have fun and enjoy life.

Secrets of the mind

Vocabulary

stay, *spend* and *pass*; *make*, *cause* and *have*; *achieve*, *carry out* and *devote*

1 Circle the correct verb.
1 Did you *stay / spend* at the match till the end?
2 Seeing friends is the best way to *spend / pass* the time on holiday.
3 We *spend / pass* one afternoon a week at my grandparents' house.
4 Studies have shown that teenagers *spend / pass* more time playing computer games than watching TV.
5 Some people prefer *staying / spending* at home to going out.
6 A lot of time has *spent / passed* since we saw each other.

2 Which verbs in the table collocate with the nouns in the box? Put the nouns in the correct column. Some can go in more than one column.

> progress   fun   patience   confusion   trouble
> a shock   peace   an effort   damage   an impact on
> changes   offence   a mistake   unhappiness

make	cause	have

3 Match the two parts of the sentences.
1 During the exam the students tried to carry out …
2 My brother's project was very good because he devoted …
3 Ella finally achieved …
4 Scientists have been carrying out …
5 Some scientists devote …
6 Football teams work hard to achieve …

A new research on what makes people happy.
B her ambition to become a doctor.
C their teacher's instructions perfectly.
D their lives to finding a cure for diseases.
E a lot of time to it.
F success in the league.

1 …………   2 …………   3 …………
4 …………   5 …………   6 …………

Unit 9

Adjectives describing personality

4 **EP** Match the adjectives with the definitions.

1 creative
2 sociable
3 adventurous
4 shy
5 ambitious
6 nervous

A Someone who wants to achieve a lot and be successful.
B Someone who is imaginative and has lots of ideas.
C Someone who is friendly and likes meeting new people.
D Someone who worries a lot and gets stressed easily.
E Someone who finds it difficult to meet new people.
F Someone who enjoys risky and challenging experiences.

5 Now choose one adjective from above to describe the people in each photograph.

Listening Part 4

▶ **10** You will hear an interview with Professor Jackson, a psychologist, talking about the science of happiness. For questions 1–7, choose the best answer (A, B or C).

1 Professor Jackson thinks surveys on happiness
   A are less accurate than other studies.
   B will be used to measure the success of governments.
   C will become less useful in the future.

2 What does Professor Jackson suggest about diet?
   A It is given more attention by happy people.
   B People feel happier if they have a good diet.
   C It has less effect on life expectancy than happiness.

3 What seems to be the relationship between standard of living and happiness?
   A People are happier now than in the past.
   B People in rich countries are getting happier.
   C People need to achieve a basic income to be happy.

4 People who buy material goods to make them happy are
   A usually dissatisfied with their purchases.
   B confusing happiness with pleasure.
   C only happy for a short time.

5 What does Professor Jackson say about the effect of relationships on happiness?
   A Having strong friendships may improve health.
   B People with a lot of friends seem to be the happiest.
   C Close friends are more important for happiness than family.

6 What do recent studies say about happiness at school?
   A People need to feel useful.
   B People need to enjoy their studies.
   C People need to have goals.

7 Professor Jackson says the easiest way to increase happiness is to
   A smile more often.
   B stop comparing yourself to others.
   C do something kind every day.

Reading and Use of English Part 3

For questions 1–8, read the text below. Use the word given in capitals at the end of some of the lines to form a word that fits in the gap **in the same line**. There is an example at the beginning (0).

Personality types

It's often said that no two people are exactly (0) ....*alike*.... , but according to one (1) .... theory, we all share one of 16 distinct personality types, which are formed by several (2) .... of personality traits.

(3) .... can be made between personality and left- or right-handedness. Most people are born with a (4) .... for one hand, and all of us are born with a personality type. Experts say that we (5) .... develop our personality type through the course of our lives in (6) .... to our (7) .... and experiences – school or work, for example. However, it should be emphasised that personality type doesn't explain everything about us and that the (8) .... of people with the same personality type can differ hugely.

LIKE
PSYCHOLOGY

COMBINE

COMPARE

PREFER

TYPICAL

RESPOND
SURROUND

BEHAVE

Reading and Use of English Part 2

EXAM ADVICE

Read the whole text when you have finished to make sure the words you have written make sense.

For questions 1–8, read the text below and think of the word which best fits each gap. Use only **one** word in each gap. There is an example at the beginning (0).

The happiest day of the year

A British psychologist says he can prove that the last Friday in June is the happiest day of the year.

Cliff Arnall, a University of Cardiff psychologist specialising (0) ....*in*........ seasonal disorders, (1) .... created a formula for finding happiness. The research looks (2) .... everything from increased outdoor activity and rising energy levels, to picnics and beach trips with families.

Mr Arnall's happiness formula depends (3) .... six factors: outdoor activity, nature, social interaction, positive memories of childhood summers, temperature, and holidays and anticipation of time off.

'At the end of June, the days are at their longest (4) .... means there are more hours of sunshine to enjoy. It's (5) .... people tend to have lots of gatherings with friends and family,' Mr Arnall said.

'Happiness is associated with many things in life and can (6) .... triggered by a variety of events. Whether it's a sunny day (7) .... a childhood memory that triggers a feeling of happiness, I think this formula proves that the path to finding happiness is very (8) .... simpler than people imagine.'

10 On the money

Grammar

Modals expressing ability

1 **Complete these sentences with** *can*, *could* **or the correct form of** *able to*. **In three of the sentences, there are two possible answers so write both.**

1 I *might be able* to give you a lift but I'm not sure yet.
2 I .... (not) swim till last year. Until then I was nervous about going in a boat.
3 I .... see Sarah in the distance. She'll be here soon.
4 I've done my maths homework but I've just had a piano lesson so I .... (not) write my history essay yet.
5 Before we moved house, I .... run from home to school in four minutes.
6 .... (you) play the guitar by the end of the course next month?
7 I .... go to last Saturday's match in the end because my friend had a spare ticket.
8 My brother .... (usually) fix the computer when it goes wrong.

as and *like*

2 **Are** *as* **and** *like* **used correctly in these sentences? Correct any mistakes and put a tick (✓) next to the sentences which are correct.**

1 As you know, this school has been here for more than 100 years. ....✓............
2 I bought Jack the same CD as you. ....
3 Tommy looks as his grandfather did at the same age. ....
4 As far as I know, there are three new players coming to training today. ....
5 I really admire him as a teacher, and I'm sure our class will learn a lot from him. ....
6 A loganberry is a bit like a raspberry but bigger. ....
7 Your hands are as cold like ice. ....
8 We didn't talk about the important things as the topic of our project. ....
9 The beginning of this film was exactly the same as the one we saw last week. ....
10 My sister's working in Italy at the moment like a tour guide. ....

Vocabulary

arrive, *get* and *reach*

1 **Circle the correct word in italics.**

1 By the time we *arrived* / (*reached*) / *got* the coast we'd been walking for four hours.
2 Did you *arrive* / *reach* / *get* in Brazil today?
3 When you *arrive* / *reach* / *get* to the sports centre, will you text me?
4 The temperature *arrived* / *reached* / *got* almost 40 degrees yesterday.
5 When Pablo *arrived* / *reached* / *got* at the hostel, the door was locked and he couldn't get in.
6 We spent ages talking about what to do but we couldn't *arrive* / *reach* / *get* a decision.

Shopping

2 Read a conversation between two friends in a sports shop and choose one word from the box for each gap. Some of the words need to be plural.

> bargain brand ~~catalogue~~ chain competitor
> counter guarantee refund sale stock

Sally: Hi Jane, fancy seeing you here looking at tennis rackets! I didn't know you played.
Jane: I've just started having lessons, and I'm thinking of asking my family for a racket for my birthday. I'm borrowing my cousin's at the moment. This shop sent us a (1) ...*catalogue*... through the post and they seem to have some good ones.
Sally: Yeah, they have some good (2) ...., though a lot of them are expensive. But they have a big (3) .... twice a year and you can often get good (4) .... then.
Jane: My dad said that as they're part of a big (5) ...., with lots of stores across the country, they're sometimes a bit cheaper than their (6) .... Anyway, what are you looking for?
Sally: I'm actually bringing a watch back. My mum got it for me here two months ago, but it's already stopped working. There's a two-year (7) .... on it and I think I'll ask for a (8) .... rather than exchange it.
Jane: Sounds like a good idea. The racket I'd like to look at doesn't seem to be in (9) ....
Sally: You never know, they might have one in the storeroom. Why don't you ask that assistant over there, by the (10) .... ?
Jane: OK! See you later.
Sally: Bye!

Phrasal verbs

3 Read the text below. Circle the correct words.

LEARNING TO MANAGE MONEY Andrew, 14

My parents give me a small allowance because they want me to get used to managing my own money. They set (**1**) *up* / off a bank account for me and they pay a small amount (**2**) *back / in* every month. When I want to go to the cinema or something like that, I take (**3**) *away / out* what I need. Sometimes I even give some (**4**) *in / away* to my best friend, because he's always running (**5**) *down / out of* money!
I can't ever take (**6**) *out / over* more money than I have in my account, so I can't get (**7**) *up / into* money debt. If I spend all my money in the first week of the month, then I have to cut (**8**) *back / off* and go (**9**) *out / without* things like chocolate bars for a while. Sometimes I sit down and add (**10**) *up / up to* how much I've spent and compare it with how much money I have, but not often!

Unit 10

Reading and Use of English Part 6

You are going to read an article about the psychology of shopping. Six sentences have been removed from the article. Choose from the sentences A–G the one which fits each gap (1–6). There is one extra sentence which you do not need to use.

Who's playing mind games with you?

Designing a shop is a science, as we found out when we did some research

A bit of retail therapy is supposed to be good for you. You stroll round the shops at leisure, try on items which catch your eye, make those purchases you've been meaning to get for ages. But who's really making the choices? You're certainly picking up the bill, but the shops could be having a bigger say than you think.

We all know how supermarkets use the smell of baking around the store to draw shoppers in, and how soothing music can make you stay longer while faster tunes are designed to keep you on the move. **1** Tim Denison, who is a retail psychologist, confirmed this increase and he let me in on some of the secrets of the retail sector.

The shops are clearly far more sophisticated than you might think. **2** In fact, this can start before you even get that far, with warm air over the doorway to encourage you in. Of course, that wouldn't work in hot countries. They have their own version with air conditioning at the entrance.

Smells are still a favourite – travel agents sometimes release a coconut odour to get you in the holiday mood. Items placed at eye level are supposed to sell better, and the end-of-aisle displays are best for persuading people to buy food they hadn't intended to. **3** You're then more likely to stop and buy something. Colours are also used successfully.

But where the art is really catching on is in the way it differentiates between women and men. A woman entering a shop might well find party clothes, with lots of frills and special materials, at the front. 'The key to effective retailing for women,' explains Tim, 'is to make the buying of clothes an engaging experience.' **4** They will be grouped not by what they are but by their style – classic or casual, for instance.

When men go shopping it's a different ball game. They want to buy a pair of jeans because their old ones have worn out. In fact, they probably want to get exactly the same jeans. **5** So menswear shops are laid out with everything in its place and men can buy what they want and go. 'We all know that men hate shopping,' says Tim, 'so what we have to do is make it as simple and spartan as we can.'

But just as the shops are becoming more sophisticated, so are the shoppers. If you're looking for a flat to buy or rent and you notice the smell of freshly brewed coffee, you're likely to get suspicious because this is an old trick to convince people it's a nice place to live. So while the mind games are targeting our subconscious, they tend to work well. **6** We don't mind spending our hard-earned cash, but we want to feel we're making the choices, not them.

A Such items are placed near each other so they can be visualised together, as an outfit.

B These kinds of techniques have been around for a while, but there's evidence that their use is growing.

C When those decisions are made for us, it can stop us from buying anything at all.

D You spend longer turning corners with awkward trolleys, so they catch your eye.

E These shoppers don't want to be faced with ideas and suggestions.

F But if they become too obvious, we're likely to resist, and things can backfire for shop-owners.

G The minute you walk through their front doors, most of your senses are attacked.

Listening Part 1

▶ 11 You will hear people talking in eight different situations. For questions 1–8, choose the best answer (A, B or C).

1. You hear a woman talking to her son. Why is she talking to him?
   A to refuse permission
   B to make a suggestion
   C to give a warning

2. You overhear a teenager talking to a shop assistant. What does he want to do?
   A get a refund
   B try something on
   C exchange something

3. You overhear two people talking. The girl dislikes
   A having to work all day.
   B working in the stock room.
   C people not being polite.

4. You hear the following on the radio. What does the man do?
   A advertise a product
   B give some advice
   C announce a decision

5. You hear two people talking about their holiday plans. What do they agree about?
   A how much cash to take
   B where to exchange their money
   C how to carry their money

6. You overhear a woman talking to a friend. The woman thinks the shop assistant was
   A well informed.
   B helpful.
   C efficient.

7. You hear a teenager talking to his friend about buying clothes online. What does he think is the main advantage?
   A You can get a good price.
   B You can avoid going to the shops.
   C You have a wide choice of styles.

8. You hear a message on an answerphone. How does the speaker feel?
   A sympathetic
   B determined
   C optimistic

Reading and Use of English Part 3

For questions 1–8, read the text below. Use the word given in capitals at the end of some of the lines to form a word that fits in the gap **in the same line**. There is an example at the beginning (0).

Designer labels

The biggest and most (0) *profitable* companies have large advertising budgets which they use to make their name familiar. When people are looking for new trainers, clothes or gadgets and have a (1) .... between two different products – one with a label they have heard of and one which by contrast is (2) .... to them – they often decide on the product whose name they recognise. It makes them think that they are buying something of (3) .... quality which they can trust. However, if they looked carefully at them, they might find the number of (4) .... between the products quite (5) .... People often willingly pay extra for the name of the designer or company without (6) .... gaining very much in quality or style. If they are (7) ...., they should therefore not be persuaded that something is better because of the label on it. But advertising is very (8) .... and, however hard people try, it is always likely to influence their decision.

PROFIT

CHOOSE

KNOW

REASON

SIMILAR
SURPRISE

ACTUAL

SENSE

EFFECT

11 Medical matters

Grammar

Relative pronouns and relative clauses

1 a Complete the sentences with the correct relative pronoun from the box.

> which   who   whose   where

1 There are a lot of after-school sports activities at my school but the people ....*who*.......... most need exercise don't go.
2 Schools .... provide relaxation classes for students get better exam results.
3 At my school there are lots of children .... parents belong to the local sports club.
4 The diet .... children had 30 or 40 years ago was much healthier.
5 The government .... job it is to promote healthy eating is not doing enough to encourage parents to change their shopping and cooking habits.
6 It's the unhealthy options on our school menu .... are always the cheapest.
7 Childhood obesity .... is now a huge problem in Europe may have a significant impact on life expectancy.
8 There aren't many sports activities available for boys .... aren't interested in football.
9 The biggest problem .... many schools have is preventing pupils from bringing unhealthy snacks into school.
10 Having a place .... children can do sports outside school is also really important.

b Add commas to the sentences containing non-defining relative clauses.

c Which relative pronouns can be replaced by *that*?

d Which relative pronouns can be omitted?

2 Match the two halves of the sentences.

1 The doctor, whose name I can't remember, ...
2 The doctor recommends that I eat less meat, ...
3 The treatment I've been having ...
4 I don't know where ...
5 People who are over the age of 50 ...
6 Supplements of vitamin C, which may help to fight infection, ...

A doesn't seem to be working very well.
B need to have a check-up every year.
C I caught this cold.
D gave me some good advice.
E should be taken during winter.
F which I will find very difficult.

1 ....   2 ....   3 ....
4 ....   5 ....   6 ....

Vocabulary

Word formation

1 **EP** What are the noun forms of these adjectives?

possible	..........*possibility*..........
satisfied	....
willing	....
helpful	....
aware	....
patient	....
able	....
experienced	....
convenient	....
accurate	....
secure	....
certain	....
happy	....
honest	....

2 Now write the negative of the adjective forms in the correct column. One word has two negative forms.

dis	im	in	un
	impossible		

Medical matters

Writing Part 1 — Developing your argument

1 Read part of the first draft of a student's answer to this essay and the teacher's comments.

> In your English class, you have been talking about people's eating habits now and in the past. Now, your English teacher has asked you to write an essay.
>
> Write an essay using all the notes and give reasons for your point of view.
>
> **Essay question**
> *Young people's diets are unhealthier today than in the past.*
>
> **Notes**
> Write about:
> 1 unhealthy snacks
> 2 cooking habits
> 3 your own idea

There is a lot of evidence to show that young people's diets are unhealthier today than in the past. **(1)** Today young people's diets are unhealthier than in the past because they eat too many unhealthy snacks. **(2)** In the past young people didn't buy so many snacks **(3)**. Young people's diets are also unhealthier because they eat too much fast food, **(4)**. Nowadays, a lot of parents don't have time for cooking, **(5)** so they buy supermarket meals to put in the microwave instead. In the past people didn't have microwaves.
On the other hand, young people's diets have improved a lot in the last 50 years. **(6)**. There is a lot of information for parents about the kinds of food they should give their children. **(7)** Young people are also taught about the importance of a good diet in school.

Teacher's comments:
- Give an example
- Explain why this is a problem
- Explain why not
- What is wrong with fast food?
- Explain why not
- Give an example
- In what way?

2 Now match the sentences/clauses from the student's second draft (A–H) to the correct part (1–7) of the essay. There is one extra sentence which does not match.

A Most tins and packets that people buy today, for example, have labels on them saying exactly what they contain.

B which is bad for their health, because this type of food isn't fresh and contains too much sugar, fat and salt.

C This means young people don't eat as much healthy food as they should and so many of them are overweight.

D For example, young people see these snacks advertised on television.

E Although many people in some countries still suffer from malnutrition, in richer countries most parents can afford to buy meat and fresh fruit for their children, which was not possible for a lot of families in the past.

F A good example of this is the fact that in many parts of the world childhood obesity has increased dramatically recently.

G because they have full-time jobs.

H because they didn't have as much money as young people today.

1 .... 2 .... 3 ....
4 .... 5 .... 6 ....
7 ....

Unit 11

Reading and Use of English Part 3

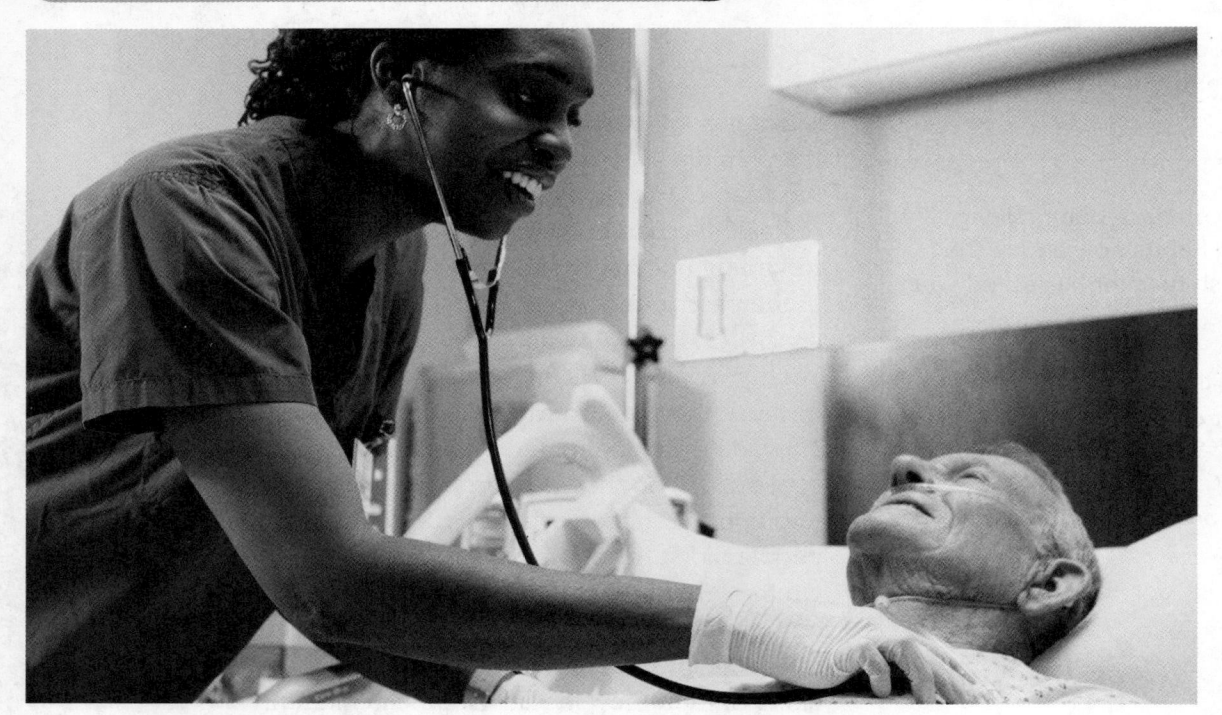

For questions 1–8, read the text below. Use the words given in capitals at the end of some of the lines to form a word that fits in the space **in the same line**. There is an example at the beginning (**0**).

Taking care of nurses

It's a nurse's (**0**) _responsibility_ to care for her patients and help them   **RESPONSIBLE**
recover from their illness. This doesn't just mean giving patients
medicine. Part of the (**1**) .... may involve giving them advice   **TREAT**
on improving their diet and exercise routines so they can increase
their (**2**) .... and avoid becoming ill again. But who looks after   **STRONG**
the well-being and (**3**) .... of nurses?   **FIT**

While trying to satisfy the demands of a busy schedule, some nurses
find it difficult to take the time to take care of themselves. This is
especially true of young, (**4**) .... nurses.   **EXPERIENCE**

Because nurses have a very (**5**) .... lifestyle and are constantly   **ACTION**
rushed off their feet, they're unlikely to need any (**6**) ....   **ADD**
exercise. However, many nurses often don't have a (**7**) ....   **BALANCE**
diet because they're too busy to eat properly during the working day.
This can mean relying on snacks instead of having (**8**) ....   **HEALTH**
meals. So some nurses may not be getting the nutrition they need to
maintain energy levels or fight off infectious diseases.

Reading and Use of English Part 4

For questions 1–6, complete the second sentence so that it has a similar meaning to the first sentence, using the word given. **Do not change the word given.** You must use between **two** and **five** words, including the word given. Here is an example (0).

Example:

0 Children's diets are not as healthy as they used to be.
MORE
Children's diets are ....*more unhealthy than*.... they used to be.

1 The doctor said I should do more exercise.
ADVISED
The doctor .... more exercise.

2 You won't lose weight unless you stop eating junk food.
IF
You won't lose weight .... eating junk food.

3 'Why don't we go for a jog?' Mike said.
SUGGESTED
Mike .... for a jog.

4 I expect people ate more vegetables in the past.
MUST
People .... in the past.

5 'I'll give you a check-up next week,' said Amy's doctor.
EXPLAINED
The doctor .... give Amy a check-up the following week.

6 Ella was so tired she couldn't study properly.
TOO
Ella .... study properly.

Listening Part 4

▶12 You will hear a high-school student interviewing a doctor as part of his research for a project on sleep. For questions 1–7, choose the best answer (**A**, **B** or **C**).

1 Compared to the past, people now sleep at night
A less heavily.
B longer than recommended.
C for a shorter time.

2 The doctor says a natural pattern of sleep includes
A one long sleep at night.
B a short sleep in the afternoon.
C frequent short sleeps.

3 Research has already shown that a lack of sleep can affect teenagers'
A long-term health.
B performance at school.
C emotional well-being.

4 What does the doctor say is to blame for teenagers not getting enough sleep?
A poor diet
B lack of exercise
C lack of discipline at home

5 What advice does the doctor give for teenagers who have trouble getting to sleep?
A read a favourite book
B listen to music
C drink hot chocolate

6 What does the doctor think schools should do?
A shorten the school day
B offer classes in the evenings
C start lessons later

7 The doctor says that you may find when you wake up
A you have forgotten a problem.
B you can see a solution to a problem.
C you think a problem is less important.

12 Animal kingdom

Grammar

Third conditional

1 Read about the day when Sara became a film extra. Complete the sentences with the correct form of the verbs in brackets.

1 Sara: If it ......*hadn't rained*...... (not rain), I ......*would have walked*...... (walk) to my dance class with Mum.

We can't walk to dance class because of the rain.

2 Sara: If the car .... (start), Mum .... (drive) me to the class.

The car won't start, so Mum can't drive me.

3 Sara: If we .... (run) faster, we .... (catch) the bus.

We didn't run fast enough.

4 Sara: If we .... (not go) to the station we .... (not see) the film crew.

A film crew!

5 Sara: If we .... (not miss) the train, the director .... (not notice) us.

Oh no, we missed the train too!

6 Sara: If it .... (be) a sunny day, I .... (not be) in a film!

I'm glad it rained that day!

wish, if only and hope

2 Complete each sentence with *wish* or *hope*.

1 I ......*hope*...... you understand what I'm trying to say.
2 My class has entered a competition and we .... we've won first prize.
3 I .... you could come to New York with us but I know your parents won't let you.
4 I .... Yusuf will be back from the match with Dad in time for dinner because Mum's cooked his favourite meal.
5 I .... I'm not disturbing you but I need to talk to you.
6 We all .... you were here because we miss you.
7 I .... someone would invent a mobile phone that would work everywhere.
8 I .... you and your family had a good time on your holiday in Thailand.
9 I .... I hadn't said exactly what I thought.
10 I .... Anton wouldn't watch TV all the time.

3 If a pair of sentences has the same meaning, put a tick (✓) next to them. If they have different meanings, rewrite the second sentence so it means the same as the first.

1. a What a pity I didn't bring my camera.
   b If only I ~~hadn't~~ brought my camera.   ....**✗** *had*......
2. a I would like the elephants to come closer.
   b I wish the elephants had come closer.   ....
3. a It's a shame we didn't see any giraffes.
   b If only we had seen some giraffes.   ....
4. a We made a lot of noise so we didn't see many animals.
   b If we had made a lot of noise, we would have seen more animals.   ....

Vocabulary

avoid, *prevent* and *protect*; *check*, *control* and *supervise*

EP Circle the correct word in each sentence.

1. The zoo keeper sometimes has to *control / prevent* people from feeding the animals.
2. My parents are going to *check / avoid* when the rainy season is before they book our holiday.
3. It's best to *prevent / avoid* going on safari during the busiest months of the year.
4. Children need to be *supervised / checked* at all times when visiting the zoo.
5. It's dangerous to ride a horse if you can't *control / supervise* it.
6. What's the best way to *protect / avoid* some rare animals from extinction?

Writing Part 2 An email

1 Look at the beginnings of five sentences below. Choose endings from A–E to give advice about visiting Yellowstone Park in the USA. There are several possible answers.

1 I'd advise you	A I'd check if any paths are closed before you set out.
2 Make sure that you	B to wear a bell.
3 The best idea is	C to carry lots of water with you.
4 You should always	D tell someone where you are going.
5 If I were you,	E walk with other people.

Example: *I'd advise you to wear a bell.*

2 Now read the email. Complete each gap with one of the sentences from Exercise 1.

To: Irena
From: Meg
📎 1 Attachment

Dear Irena

You said in your last email that you're going to Yellowstone Park in the USA with your family for a holiday. I went there last year and I know you'll all have a good time.

But don't forget that Yellowstone is bear country. While you're walking, make sure you all make a lot of noise, which frightens the bears away. **(1)** .... Some parts of the park are shut in spring and early summer. **(2)** ....

The other thing to remember is that most of the park is wild. It can be dangerous to be in too small a group. **(3)** .... Even if you are in a big group, it's really important that you all plan your route carefully. **(4)** .... Finally, it can get very hot. **(5)** ....

Here's a photo of me in Yellowstone. It's a beautiful place.

Love Meg

Unit 12

Reading and Use of English Part 5

You are going to read an article from a magazine about a holiday in Africa. For questions 1–6, choose the answer (A, B, C or D) which you think fits best according to the text.

African Safari

Martin Symington went on a camping safari holiday with his wife and three teenagers

We stood silently under the stars, just metres from our tent, hardly daring to breathe. Adam, one of the camp staff, swept a torch beam across a clearing where four impala stood, panicky on their nimble legs. Could they sense the danger they were in? Did they know, as we did, that a female leopard lay under a thorn bush?

She sprang. Four shadowy shapes bounced into the woods. Had the leopard made a successful kill? We all had our theories, but in truth the whole scene had taken place too quickly, and in insufficient light, for any of us to be sure. Now we understood why we had been warned not to go out of our tent after dark, except when accompanied by a staff member. If fact, we had been on our way from the tent to the supper-time camp-fire when Adam's torch had unexpectedly caught the leopard's glinting green eyes. Half an hour later we had a tale to outdo most told around the fire. 'This has got to be the best nightlife in the world,' replied Toby, when some middle-aged, fellow safari enthusiast asked him how he was enjoying his holiday.

So much for the assortment of self-appointed experts who doubted that safaris and teenagers would be a workable mix. True, this is a difficult age, with adolescents beginning to sense that they are too old for family holidays. But nor did ours want to return to beach resorts with the kind of 'teen clubs' they wouldn't be seen dead in. So, my wife Hennie and I reckoned, if we were going to have one really good family holiday, why not Africa?

Our holiday began with a flight to Arusha airport, then a long drive to West Kilimanjaro Camp – a semi-permanent gathering of explorer-style tents near the base of the great volcano which was to tease us with rare glimpses of her snowy summit which is 5,895 metres high.

Next we took to the hot African sky in a small plane and headed south. Unlike in West Kilimanjaro, there is no human population in the Ruaha other than a lodge for the park rangers, and four small safari camps. We chose to stay at Mdonya Old River Camp because this is one that avoids luxuries such as soft beds and fluffy towels; these, to my mind, can become obstacles to connecting with nature in the raw. Instead, the five of us shared a simple, yet adequate, tent at the edge of a dried-up sand river.

If there was one disappointment about the wildlife viewing in Tanzania, it was that game drives are not permitted in any of the country's national parks after dusk. But if anything, this made our night-time meeting *line* with the leopard and impala outside our tent even more special, bringing home to us the rewards of staying at camps where there are no fences, distractions or even electricity.

By day we mixed game drives with walks through the bush under the protection of our guide Esau for the time we spent in Ruaha. He taught us about bush safety: stay attentive and at a distance from the wildlife, and always stand still if you see an animal approaching you. We spotted only plant-eating animals – elephant, zebra and a pair of giraffes – but we all listened carefully to his repeated message to 'remember that you will see less than one per cent of what sees you'.

Our final hop was over to Zanzibar where we sailed out to a sandbank, swam through bright yellow and pink-and-blue fish and watched a crimson sunset. And we concluded that if there is one family holiday that will have undying teen appeal, it is a safari.

1 How did the family feel when they were sitting round the camp-fire?

   A interested in the stories of the other campers
   B proud of what they had seen earlier
   C sorry they had disturbed the leopard
   D annoyed they didn't know what happened in the end

2 Why did the writer and his wife decide to choose a safari holiday in Africa?

   A They didn't want to be with other families.
   B They wanted their children to learn some independence.
   C They wanted to do something different from usual.
   D They were advised that teenagers often enjoy safaris.

3 They chose the Mdonya Old River Camp because

   A there was water nearby.
   B it wasn't easy to get to.
   C the tents were of good quality.
   D it was fairly basic.

4 'this' in line 51 refers to

   A the dusk
   B a rule
   C their disappointment
   D a plan

5 What did Esau warn them about?

   A There were many more animals than they could actually see.
   B They should move slowly if an animal came towards them.
   C They shouldn't go into the bush alone on foot.
   D Some animals were more dangerous than others.

6 Which of the following describes how the writer felt about the holiday?

   A unsure whether they would come back again
   B frustrated they hadn't seen more animals
   C relieved they hadn't been attacked
   D satisfied the children had enjoyed it

Animal kingdom

Listening Part 2

▶13 You will hear a woman called Kirsty Willis, who works in a zoo, giving a talk to students about careers with animals. For questions 1–10, complete the sentences with a word or short phrase.

Careers with animals

Working in a zoo

You have more chance of getting a job if you have (1) ....

You will have little (2) .... with the animals.

You must be good at (3) ....

It's ideal for people who like to have daily (4) ....

Working in an aquarium

You should be able to handle a (5) ....

You will (6) .... at the end of the day!

Working as a vet

Animals often have a (7) .... attitude towards vets.

You need to be able to (8) .... well.

Working as a trainer

Most opportunities are in (9) ....

A typical day lasts (10) .... hours.

51

13 House space

Grammar

Causative *have* and *get*

1 a What does the woman need to have done? Complete the sentences with the correct form of the verbs from the box.

| clean   remove   replace   ~~fix~~   cut |

1 She needs *to have/get* the roof *fixed*.
2 She wants .... the windows ....
3 She is going .... the hedge ....
4 She would like .... the rubbish ....
5 She thinks she should .... the gate ....

b What has the woman had done? Write sentences.

6 *She has had the roof fixed.*
7 ....
8 ....
9 ....
10 ....

Expressing obligation and permission

2 Circle the correct words in each sentence.

1 *You're not supposed to* / *You are allowed to* bring your dog into this building but it won't matter if no one sees him.
2 My brother *needn't have bought* / *didn't need to buy* a washing machine for his new apartment. He'll have to sell it on eBay.
3 My parents *aren't allowed to have* / *won't let me have* a TV in my bedroom.
4 You *don't have to* / *mustn't* carry that heavy box up the stairs. There's a lift over there.
5 We *can't* / *needn't* play loud music after 11 p.m., or the neighbours will complain.
6 You *shouldn't have* / *couldn't have* left the door unlocked. Go back and lock it!
7 The builders *were supposed to* / *had to* finish work on 21st June but the kitchen isn't ready yet.
8 *Don't let your little brother* / *Your little brother doesn't have to* climb that tree. It's not safe.
9 You *should* / *must* lock the door when you go out or thieves could get in.
10 My mum says we *should* / *are allowed to* have the party at our house if we promise to clear up afterwards.

at, *in* and *on* to express location

3 Complete the sentences with the correct preposition: *in*, *on*, *at*.

1 Our apartment is .... the first floor.
2 I'll meet you .... the entrance to the cinema.
3 The airport is .... the outskirts of the city.
4 The building doesn't look very exciting .... the outside but it's amazing inside.
5 You can park .... the back of the hotel.
6 We put all the furniture .... the middle of the room when we were decorating.
7 There's plenty of storage space .... the basement.
8 There's a huge mirror .... the top of the stairs.

Vocabulary

Collocations describing where you live

EP Cross out the option in *italics* which is NOT correct.

1 The sports centre in our town is *conveniently / comfortably / ideally* located.
2 The neighbourhood where my family live used to be quite run-down but in the last few years it has become much more *desirable / fashionable / likeable*.
3 My parents *converted / installed / turned* the smallest bedroom in our house into a shower room.
4 My bedroom *overlooks / looks onto / gives an overview of* the garden.
5 My cousin's apartment is quite small but there's *enough / sufficient / convenient* space for one person.
6 My friend's family's house is furnished very *luxuriously / expensively / richly*.
7 When my brother first moved into a flat on his own, he could only afford *poor / cheap / second-hand* furniture.
8 The design of the kitchen is very *simple / stylish / well equipped*.
9 Unfortunately there isn't much *room / place / space* for us to have a party at home.
10 The main square is a good *place / location / area* for meeting friends.

Listening Part 4

▶ 14 You will hear a journalist talking on the radio about adults in their 20s and 30s who still live with their parents. For questions 1–7, choose the best answer (A, B or C).

1 The survey shows that the European country with the lowest number of 'boomerang kids' is

   A France.
   B Sweden.
   C the UK.

2 In southern Europe young adults continue to live at home because of

   A low salaries.
   B close family ties.
   C a shortage of affordable housing.

3 In the USA people are leaving home later because

   A they are getting married later.
   B they have to pay off student debts.
   C their relationships with their parents are good.

4 Young adults living at home say the main advantage is

   A being able to save up.
   B having someone to do their washing and ironing.
   C being free from responsibilities.

5 One disadvantage mentioned by 'boomerang kids' in the survey is

   A the lack of time spent alone.
   B worrying what people think of them.
   C being treated like a child.

6 Having adult children at home can be a problem for parents because it can

   A restrict their freedom.
   B be expensive.
   C make them tired.

7 The most common source of conflict between parents and their adult children are

   A household chores.
   B mealtimes.
   C financial arrangements.

Unit 13

Writing Part 2 — Adding detail

1 Read some sentences from an article a student wrote about her grandparents' kitchen. Then match them to the type of detail they provide (A–F).

Type of detail
A providing a description
B making a comparison
C giving an opinion
D giving an example
E providing facts
F describing feelings

1 ....   2 ....   3 ....
4 ....   5 ....   6 ....

2 Now look at this examination task. Which of the sentences in Exercise 1 do you think would be relevant for this article? Tick them.

My favourite room

Tell us about your favourite room and why it's special for you.

The best article will be published in next month's magazine.

3 Plan your answer for this task. What type of detail would you include?

My favourite room

Facts?

Description?

Feelings?

Opinions?

1. I always associate the kitchen with my grandmother.
2. The house was built in 1910 and the kitchen was extended in the 1970s.
3. My grandfather prefers to eat in the dining room because the chairs are more comfortable but my grandmother thinks it's too formal in there.
4. There are usually some flowers from the garden on the table and the smell of something wonderful cooking in the ancient oven.
5. It's difficult to choose my favourite dish but most people agree that my grandmother's fruit cake is delicious.
6. She's a very generous person; she makes jam for all her neighbours and gives them cherries and strawberries from her garden.

Reading and Use of English Part 1

For questions 1–8, read the text below and decide which answer (A, B, C or D) best fits each gap. There is an example at the beginning (0).

0   A knowledge   **B idea**   C understanding   D suggestion

A writer's room

It may not look like an office, but that's the point. The (0) .... of having to work all day in an office would mean I never went there. So there are no filing cabinets or piles of mail and no distracting shelves of books.

All over the flat there are photographs I've taken of (1) .... countries I've visited; in here they're (2) .... of New Zealand – and I keep my travelling hat and my travelling bag hanging here to make me (3) .... that I could pack up and leave at any (4) .... I can't, but it's nice to (5) ....

If I'm doing serious writing, I prefer to be in here at night, typing on a laptop because I don't have a desk and have no (6) .... for one. When I injured my back, I saved up and bought the monster black leather chair. I try not to (7) .... anyone else sit in it, because they usually (8) .... to get out again – it's just too comfortable.

1   A various   B broad   C general   D widespread
2   A completely   B especially   C extensively   D primarily
3   A consider   B dream   C imagine   D expect
4   A moment   B event   C date   D occasion
5   A invent   B pretend   C suppose   D believe
6   A hope   B obligation   C demand   D desire
7   A permit   B allow   C let   D authorise
8   A disagree   B refuse   C reject   D deny

14 Fiesta!

Grammar

The passive

1 Complete the newspaper article below by putting the verbs in brackets into the correct form of the passive.

Join us at the Festival of Dance

A dance festival (**1**) *has been held* (*hold*) in our town every summer since 2005. It (**2**) .... (*organise*) every year by three local schools and each child (**3**) .... (*give*) the opportunity to take part in a performance, competition or street parade.
This year's festival will take place on 15 July and will be bigger than ever because £3,000 (**4**) .... (*raise*) for the prizes and there's more to come, we hope. Last year, 15 prizes of £100 (**5**) .... (*award*) but this year there will be at least 30 prizes. At last summer's festival, a local boy, Marcus Aston, (**6**) .... (*choose*) to go into a national competition. It (**7**) .... (*hope*) that other children (**8**) .... (*offer*) that chance this year.
At the end of the day, there will be a special performance by the City Schools Dance Troupe, which (**9**) .... (*form*) in 2006 and has won many prizes. They can also (**10**) .... (*see*) later in the summer at the Victoria Hall and the Thames Festival.
Plans (**11**) .... (*already make*) for next year's festival so if you would like to help, please get in touch via the website (www.dancewithus.co.uk). If you would like your name (**12**) .... (*add*) to the mailing list, you can also do that on the website.

The passive with reporting verbs

2 Rewrite the newspaper headlines as sentences, using the verb in brackets. You will need to add some extra words.

1 **WORLD'S MOST FAMOUS BOY BAND TO SPLIT UP AFTER WORLD TOUR**

The world's most famous boy band is expected to split up after their/a world tour. (*expect*)

2 **New Waterpark Will Probably Be Built Next Year**

....
.... (*think*)

3 **NEW TEAM HAS BEEN SELECTED**

It ....
.... (*report*)

4 **FEDERER IS THE BEST TENNIS PLAYER EVER**

Federer ....
.... (*consider*)

5 **Report Proves Chocolate Is Good For Your Brain**

Chocolate ....
.... (*report*)

6 **BONES FOUND ON BEACH BELONGED TO DINOSAUR**

It ....
.... (*believe*)

Writing Part 1 An essay

1 Read the exam task below and the student answer. Write *this, them, these, those* or *it* in each gap. In some gaps, more than one answer is possible.

> In your English class you have been talking about music events at school. Now, your English teacher has asked you to write an essay for homework.
> Write an essay using **all** the notes and give reasons for your point of view.
>
> Essay question
> *Students should organise regular music events at their school.*
> *Do you agree?*
>
> Notes
> Write about:
> 1 who could take part
> 2 whether students could learn something
> 3 .... (your own idea)
>
> Write your **essay** in 140–190 words.

Music is an important part of school life. Some people think students should organise music events at their school. **(1)** ......*These*........ might be ones in which students themselves play, or visits by professional musicians.

On the one hand, there are several reasons why holding events such as school concerts is beneficial. **(2)** .... can help develop students' confidence and give **(3)** .... a chance to learn how to deal with the stress of performing in public. Talented students can show their classmates what they are capable of.

Nevertheless, some people might think that **(4)** .... is not a useful way of spending valuable school time. People like **(5)** .... might say that unless all the students are interested in music, it is unfair to ask **(6)** .... to join in, because they might not learn much.

However, if students themselves are in charge, **(7)** .... can allow pupils of all ages and abilities to participate. Even **(8)** .... who are unable to play an instrument can help with the organisation and planning. Therefore, on balance, I agree that students should be involved in organising music events at school.

2 What is the student's own idea in their essay?

3 Choose a word or phrase from the list below to complete the student's essay plan.

disadvantages of students organising regular music events
conclusion
recommendation for future music events
introduction
advantages of students organising regular music events at school
description of a music event

Essay plan
Paragraph 1 ...
Paragraph 2 ...
Paragraph 3 ...
Paragraph 4 ...

4 Now write your answer to the question below. Use your own plan or a similar plan to the one in Exercise 3.

> In your English class you have been talking about drama events at school. Now, your English teacher has asked you to write an essay for homework.
> Write an essay using **all** the notes and give reasons for your point of view.
>
> Essay question
> *Students should organise regular drama events at their school.*
> *Do you agree?*
>
> Notes
> Write about:
> 1 who could take part
> 2 whether students could learn something
> 3 .... (your own idea)
>
> Write your **essay** in 140–190 words.

Unit 14

Vocabulary

Word formation – suffixes

EP Add suffixes to these words to make personal nouns. Then underline the word which is the odd one out in each case.

1. electric .... politics ....
   photograph .... music ....

2. account .... pharmacy ....
   psychology .... economy ....

3. fish .... entertain ....
   bank .... support ....

4. lecture .... produce ....
   manufacture .... investigate ....

5. history .... library ....
   sports .... comedy ....

6. contest .... inhabit ....
   assist .... employ ....

Listening Part 3

▶ 15 You will hear five short extracts in which people are talking about something they are going to celebrate. For questions 1–5, choose from the list (A–H) what each person is going to celebrate. Use the letters only once. There are three extra letters which you do not need to use.

A a birthday
B the return of a friend
C a place on a course
D a move to a new flat
E the end of a school year
F a pass in a driving test
G a win in a competition
H the arrival of a new teacher

Speaker 1 [1]
Speaker 2 [2]
Speaker 3 [3]
Speaker 4 [4]
Speaker 5 [5]

Reading and Use of English Part 7

You are going to read some texts about different festivals. For questions 1–10, choose from the texts (A–E). The texts may be chosen more than once.

Which text mentions

specific rules for some events?	1
the fact that there is no other similar festival?	2
a range of themes within a festival?	3
a regional variation?	4
a suggestion for getting a good view?	5
a festival which has been lengthened?	6
a lack of cooperation posing a problem?	7
a festival's aim to attract people who would not normally attend such an event?	8
reduced interest in a particular tradition?	9
the origins of a festival?	10

Festivals around the world

A Festival of Candelaria

The festival which takes place in Puno each year is one of the largest, longest and most extravagant celebrations in fiesta-mad Peru. So many local dance clubs now compete that the contest is spread over two weeks instead of one as in the past. There is nothing casual about these competitions. Groups must have precise numbers of participants, depending on the dance, and perform for exactly eight minutes in front of a packed stadium of transfixed spectators. After competing, many groups just keep on dancing in the narrow streets of the town.

Fiesta!

B The Edinburgh Festival

Late summer is the only period in the calendar when the cultural focus of Great Britain really shifts away from London to Scotland. For those four weeks, television crews normally based in London send their researchers searching frantically for stories and celebrities in Edinburgh. What draws the attention of the international arts world is the extraordinary cultural mix that is the Edinburgh Festival. The scale and range of its ingredients make it unique. Hundreds of events are free, many take place in the street and the festival has always recognised the vital need to involve people with no money and little experience of the arts.

C The Pushkar Fair

Once a year the Pushkar Fair takes place in India's state of Rajasthan. For five days, approximately 20,000 camels are dressed up, paraded, entered into beauty contests, raced and traded. A huge carnival is held, with musicians, magicians, dancers, acrobats, snake charmers and carousel rides to entertain the crowd. And there are camels as far as the eye can see of course. Unfortunately, camels aren't the friendliest of animals and can be obstinate creatures. More than a few camel traders seem to struggle handling their animals, who aren't interested in charming potential buyers, or even in standing up. An excellent way to witness the spectacle of the camel fair is from above by booking a ride in a hot-air balloon.

D Notting Hill Carnival

West London comes alive to the sights, sounds and colour of the Caribbean on the last weekend in August. The event has come a long way since 1964 when the local Afro-Caribbean community took a small steel band procession onto the streets. In recent years, more than two million people have taken to the streets of West London, making it second only to the Rio Carnival in size. The costumed parades form the backbone of the carnival, hoping to impress the judges with their interpretation of a chosen topic: aliens and the Wild West are just a couple of the storylines to look out for.

E The Moon Festival

'We've been working every day now for the last 60 days,' said Johnny Chan. 'We've made about three million mooncakes so far.' Mooncakes mean the Mid-Autumn Festival, or Moon Festival, which lasts for three days. The Kee Wah bakery in Hong Kong makes dozens of different types of mooncakes. 'The Cantonese-style cakes have a shiny finish, and are filled with a lotus seed paste,' said Johnny Chan. 'In the northern regions, the cakes are less sweet and are often filled with nuts or even meat,' he added. But despite their central role in the Mid-Autumn Festival, Mr Chan said that mooncake orders had declined over recent years. Part of the reason, he said, was that people think mooncakes are bad for them and prefer low-fat, low-sugar ones, but also the Moon Festival was becoming more commercialised and people focused more on the exchange of gifts.

Answer key

1 A family affair

Grammar

1. 2 haven't written   3 've/have been working
   4 've/have met   5 have invited   6 has improved
   7 haven't had   8 's/has gone   9 's/has phoned
   10 have/'ve been looking after   11 have been playing
   12 have/'ve been writing   13 have/'ve sent   14 've/have been wondering   15 've/have been doing

2. 2 What time have you been getting up every day?
   3 Have you bought anything?
   4 Have you been learning how to cook Spanish food?
   5 How many times have you eaten paella?
   6 Have you seen any films in Spanish yet?

Vocabulary

1. 2 made   3 make   4 do   5 make   6 do   7 made
   8 did   9 make   10 make

2. 2 impatient   3 aggressive   4 disorganised
   5 understanding   6 unreliable   7 enthusiastic

3. 2 clear up   3 worn out   4 go for   5 pick me up
   6 went on

Writing Part 2

I definately [definitely] think that teenage year's [years] should be the best in everyones [everyone's] life because you can have fun and you have fewer problems than adults [add full stop]. teenagers [capital T] Teenagers know how to have a good time. Most teenagers have a lot of freinds [friends] and they discuss things that they are interested in. Teenagers have to be in fashion, [add comma] wearing up-to-date cloths [clothes] and listening to modern music. They also like to do sports and compete in matchs [matches]. But teenager's [teenagers'] parents sometimes have a difficult time and they dont [don't] understand why? . [full stop, not question mark] Wouldnt [Wouldn't] you feel angry if someone went into your room without permission.? [question mark, not full stop] So do teenagers. Teenagers stop thinking like children as they grow up and their believes [beliefs] and their interests change. My opinion is that teenage years are magical and Id [I'd] like to stay a teenager forever.

Listening Part 3

1 B   2 H   3 C   4 F   5 D

Track 02

Speaker 1: Every year my family get together and go down to the river for a picnic. There's usually about 12 of us – kids and grown-ups. We always do the same thing and this year I said I wasn't going. But my parents insisted because they said it would look rude. I wouldn't have minded if it was just the afternoon but I wasn't looking forward to the whole day. When I got there though my cousin had brought a couple of her friends and we sat together. I had a good time but I would still have preferred to stay at home.

Speaker 2: Every year someone in my family arranges a day out in London for all of us. This year my mum and I did it and we chose to go to a musical. It was difficult to find a show that would appeal to everyone and we were a bit worried that my granny or my cousins wouldn't like it, as in my family everyone says what they think. So when everyone said they'd had a great time, we knew we'd made the right choice. Nobody complained, even when we missed the train home and we had to wait an hour in the station.

Speaker 3: Last weekend my aunt and uncle and cousins were staying and we decided to go out for the day. We were going to the seaside but we hadn't gone far when we drove past the zoo and my cousins said they wanted to go in. So we decided we'd go in for an hour and then carry on to the seaside. But there was so much to see that we stayed there all day. My mum and dad and my granny really aren't keen on zoos and were looking forward to a day on the beach but the rest of us didn't mind at all.

Speaker 4: My sister's birthday's in the summer so we usually go out somewhere for the day. She said she wanted to go to a theme park this year, which was good for me as I don't usually want to do what she suggests. It's a new park quite near where I live. I only went on half the rides I wanted to because it's huge. The whole park shut at six – I suppose because it was getting dark. It didn't matter though because Mum and Dad said we can go again. They enjoyed sitting in the café and reading the newspapers.

Speaker 5: Last Sunday I went to the seaside with my family. My brother and sister are older than me and they didn't really want to come but I persuaded them as otherwise it would have been a bit boring with Mum, Dad and my grandparents. When we got there, we had a swim in the sea and a lovely picnic which my granny made. <u>We agreed that we'd take a boat out in the afternoon but when we went to get one they were all out, which was a real shame</u>. Unfortunately, we hadn't realised we needed to book. So we just went for another swim and then came home.

Reading and Use of English Part 7

1 E 2 C 3 D 4 E 5 B 6 A 7 B 8 D 9 C 10 B

2 Leisure and pleasure

Grammar

1 2 most 3 riskiest 4 much 5 well 6 less
7 far 8 least

2 3 Tennis is the ~~more~~ hardest sport to learn.
4 ✓
5 It's less ~~easier~~ easy to learn a new sport as you get older.
6 For me, playing computer games is the ~~more~~ most relaxing way to spend my free time.
7 Joining a sports club can help people to become ~~more~~ healthier.
8 I am the fittest now ~~than~~ that I have ever been in my life. / I am ~~the fittest~~ fitter now than I have ever been in my life.

3 1 amazing 2 irritating 3 interested 4 embarrassing
5 disappointed 6 relaxing

4 to amuse, amusement; to confuse, confusion; to embarrass, embarrassment; to exhaust, exhaustion; to excite, excitement; to relax, relaxation; to shock, shock; to worry, worry

Writing Part 2

1 1 I enjoy playing it with all my friends because it's really exciting.
2 Any number of people can play but it's more fun with between six and eight players.
3 My favourite game is called 'Pom Pom Home' and I've been playing it since I was 5.
4 During the holidays we play for hours and we get home completely exhausted.
5 To rescue someone you have to run and touch 'home' and then you have to run away quickly before you get caught.
6 It's basically quite similar to 'Hide and Seek' but it's just a bit more complicated and active.
7 I love it when my big brother plays with us because he's a fast runner and he always rescues me if I get caught.
8 It's different every time we play because there are so many places where we can hide.

2 A: Sentences 3, 4 and 6   B: Sentences 2 and 5
C: Sentences 1, 7 and 8

Vocabulary

1 take up: an offer, a sport
start up: a business, a machine
make up: a story, an excuse
sum up: a story, the main points of an argument

2 1 B 2 E 3 C 4 F 5 A 6 D

3 2 go off 3 showing off 4 cut off 5 let us off
6 put off

Listening Part 4

1 B 2 B 3 A 4 A 5 C 6 B 7 A

Answer key: Unit 3

▶ Track 03

Interviewer: So Toby, how did you get into playing chess?

Toby: Well, I started playing with my dad when I was about 11 and I joined my club four years ago when my mom found an article in a local newspaper about <u>the team from our local chess club winning a national tournament</u>. My mom thought I would learn a lot from these guys. Now I'm one of the best players. All my opponents are much older than me but I'm used to it because it's like that everywhere. Anyway there are not too many players my age.

Interviewer: Playing chess on the Internet is very popular now, isn't it? Would you recommend that to new players?

Toby: I used to play chess on the Internet a lot and it was good up to a point. <u>But I don't any more because I found my game wasn't developing</u>. Anyway, there's nothing like the thrill of playing face to face. It's more exciting and more challenging.

Interviewer: Has watching the grandmasters play helped to develop your game?

Toby: Oh, definitely. Veselin Topalov is my favourite player of all time. He's an aggressive player and risks everything to win, and <u>he doesn't mind sacrificing pieces if he has to</u>. Sometimes I think he's going to lose and then I'm really surprised when he wins.

Interviewer: So what's the secret of your success? How do you decide which moves to make?

Toby: When making a move, I normally go on intuition. I'll look at the position and say, '<u>Which move looks comfortable to me?</u>' After that, I choose about three moves and analyse them. I play some variations in my head. What would the position be after three moves or five moves? I look at the plans of the opponent to see if I have to do something against them or not. There is no best way to play a position. It depends on the player. But most of the time, it's just a question of knowing when to make an aggressive move and when to play a defensive move. It comes with experience.

Interviewer: Do you think you'll ever get to be a grand master yourself?

Toby: At the moment my ambition is to be ranked inside the top 100 players younger than 21 in the US Chess Federation. I'm currently ranked in the top 150 but I don't see my future career in chess.

Interviewer: Why's that?

Toby: Well, for one thing, <u>I don't think I have the personality you need to be one of the top players</u>. I probably could, if I really put a lot of effort into it, be a chess trainer but it doesn't pay well. So it's better for me to play for fun.

Interviewer: Experts always recommend that parents teach their children chess to help them learn about logic. Do you think that's useful?

Toby: Yes. I think chess can teach you a lot of things. <u>You learn how to read a person by analysing the way they play chess</u>. You find out what kind of person they are; whether they're creative or analytical. For example, some people's body language also helps you to see if they are confident or worried but the best players are very controlled.

Interviewer: Some people say that a game of chess is like the game of life. Do you agree with that?

Toby: No, I don't think chess is like life. I mean in some ways I suppose you could say it's similar. Many people set themselves targets and plan ahead for the future, for example. But in my mind, it's really important to separate chess and life because <u>in chess you can plan every move you make and you have a fairly good idea of what will happen next</u>. And that's not true in life.

Interviewer: OK, we'll take a break now and …

Reading and Use of English Part 2

1 who/that   2 in/with   3 there   4 because/as/or/since   5 to   6 be   7 with   8 up

Reading and Use of English Part 4

1 wasn't/was not as expensive as
2 was disappointing for   3 because/since she took
4 like/enjoy hockey as much   5 is the least interesting
6 found the race very/really exciting

3 Happy holidays?

Grammar

1 2 were still looking; stopped   3 met; were going
4 sat; didn't eat; talked   5 woke up; were travelling
6 crossed; began   7 reached; knew
8 arrived; weren't waiting; took

2 2 had been trying 3 had owned 4 had been feeling
5 'd/had forgotten 6 'd/had been standing up

3 2 had ever been skiing 3 had been looking 4 were driving 5 started 6 got 7 wasn't/was not 8 said 9 went 10 got 11 looked 12 had been snowing

4 2 in 3 on 4 on 5 at 6 on 7 in 8 on 9 In 10 at

Vocabulary

1 2 poisonous 3 scientific 4 risky 5 fashionable 6 energetic 7 dramatic 8 adventurous 9 industrial 10 thoughtless 11 competitive 12 natural

2 Across: 4 activity 6 overnight 10 voyages 11 travel

Down: 1 backpacking 2 flight 3 cruise 5 journey 7 hostels 8 tour 9 way 11 trip

3 respond – responsible   storm – stormy
mystery – mysterious   mass – massive
doubt – doubtful   emotion – emotional
wealth – wealthy   access – accessible
predict – predictable

4 1 doubtful 2 wealthy 3 massive 4 accessible 5 stormy 6 emotional 7 mysterious 8 responsible 9 predictable

Listening Part 1

1 B 2 C 3 C 4 B 5 A 6 C 7 B 8 A

▶ Track 04

Presenter: One. You overhear someone talking to a tour guide.

Tourist: I just wanted to say, yesterday evening, when we went round the town, sightseeing, it was really good to have you show us everything and tell us where to go and what to do. I know later in the week we're going on another tour which is in the afternoon this time. So it'll be hot and I think it would be a good idea to have a break and get a drink in a café in the middle of the tour. It was OK yesterday because it was evening but I don't think I can manage to walk round for two hours in the heat.

Presenter: Two. You hear a girl talking to a friend about a place she visited on holiday with her family.

Girl: It's full of families with very young children, so there wasn't really very much for me to do. I did nearly out of space in my suitcase, though, because my parents gave me some spending money and I decided to get stuff for all my friends in the souvenir places. I spent hours wandering the streets going in and out of the souvenir places choosing things. Apart from that, there's not really much else to do. One day we got a bus into the surrounding countryside but, to be honest, it was a bit dull. There was a cinema, but nothing on worth watching!

Presenter: Three. You overhear two people talking about a holiday.

Man: Well, the holiday could have been better.

Woman: Oh, it wasn't that bad. I mean, when I realised our flight was going to be held up because of fog, I thought, 'Oh no, that's when the bags get on the wrong plane and go to the wrong place'.

Man: I know. I was worried too. I hate not having all my things.

Woman: But we were lucky there.

Man: Not so lucky with the hotel though.

Woman: Our room was OK.

Man: Well, I'm not surprised it wasn't fully booked even at the busiest time of year. I won't go back there again.

Presenter: Four. You hear a boy talking to his father on the phone.

Boy: Hi Dad! You know I said I wasn't playing in the match after school this afternoon? Well someone's dropped out, so they need me after all. The minibus is outside school right now and we're leaving in an hour. The teacher said Jim could run home to get some spare sports kit for me – he lives just round the corner and I can borrow his brother's boots. So do you think you could come and get me at six instead of three today? I'll be at Jim's house – the white one next to the petrol station – you can't miss it and his mum says it's OK.

Presenter: Five. You hear two teenagers talking about a TV programme they saw.

Boy: Did you see that documentary about Africa on TV yesterday?

Girl: Yeah, it wasn't bad, was it? Not sure about the music, though.

Boy: I quite liked it, actually. I liked that guy who presented it, too.

Girl: Gary Brown? Well, if you can stay awake while he's talking, I suppose. I wonder how they got all those pictures of the lion families – that must be so hard to do!

Answer key: Unit 4

Boy: <u>Some of those shots were amazing.</u> The babies are cool to watch, aren't they, jumping about all over the place?

Girl: Yeah, they were so cute! I loved that bit.

Presenter: Six. You hear the following announcement on a train.

Announcer: This is the 4.15 service to Birmingham. <u>This is to inform passengers travelling on this train that there will be two extra stops as stated on the departure board in the station.</u> This is because the train which was due to depart for Birmingham at 12 minutes past four was cancelled. Passengers due to travel on that train were told to catch this one instead.

This train is usually a non-stop service so we apologise for a slight delay in arriving at our destination. We also apologise to those passengers who were due to catch the earlier train.

Presenter: Seven. You hear a brother and a sister talking about a car journey they are going on.

Girl: So, we're leaving really early, Mum says. She thinks we could be there by mid-afternoon.

Boy: Great, not like last time, then.

Girl: Yes, all that traffic! Tomorrow won't be like that at all, she says. But you know how Mum and Dad don't like to stop very often? We'd better take something extra with us just in case. I'll ask if we can make some sandwiches now so we'll be ready.

Boy: I'm sure she's already thought of that.

Girl: Maybe … <u>And I've got a new magazine specially for the trip – it'll be good to have a few hours to read it in!</u>

Presenter: Eight. You hear two teenagers talking about something that happened on a train journey.

Boy: Hi, Tara. How was the train journey with your dad?

Girl: Well, it went really fast because I started talking to a boy sitting opposite us, Mark – he was with his dad too. I was telling him all about the new skate park, you know?

Boy: So, he must have been interested if he kept listening.

Girl: He was cool. The thing is I talked a lot about all the tricks I can do. We swapped contact details and when I checked online, it turns out he's a really good skater. I was a bit ashamed of myself as I didn't give him a chance to say very much, so I had no idea.

Reading and Use of English Part 3

1 unusually 2 natural 3 remarkable 4 risky 5 friendly
6 memorable 7 successfully 8 thrilling

4 Food, glorious food

Grammar

1 1 B 2 B 3 A 4 B 5 C 6 B 7 B 8 A 9 A 10 C

2 3 little → few
4 ✓
5 such long time → such a long time
6 ✓
7 many → much
8 so good as → as good as
9 much more better → much better
10 isn't → aren't

Vocabulary

1 2 elaborate 3 diet 4 food 5 simple
6 Convenience 7 filling 8 shortage 9 food
10 meal

2 1 protein 2 spinach 3 dairy 4 seaweed 5 junk
6 Herbs 7 fat 8 canteen

H	B	A	N	A	N	S	J	F
S	M	A	N	P	P	P	U	A
E	P	R	O	T	E	I	N	D
A	D	L	E	L	O	N	K	A
W	H	E	R	B	S	A	A	I
E	R	A	F	E	A	C	N	R
E	Y	A	A	T	E	H	P	Y
D	E	T	T	A	R	G	A	E
S	C	A	N	T	E	E	N	S

Writing Part 2

1 E 2 C 3 A 4 D 5 B

Reading and Use of English Part 4

1 instead of going   2 advised me to have / advised having   3 were too few   4 doesn't have / hasn't got enough   5 isn't any / is/'s no fish left   6 isn't as good as

Listening Part 2

1 responsibility   2 quality   3 team   4 ingredients
5 review   6 celebration   7 detail   8 500   9 seasonal
10 September

▶ **Track 05**

Interviewer: Today, in our series about different career options for teenagers, we welcome Noah Beesdale, who is 17 years old and has just started training as a chef. Tell us a bit about what it's like, Noah.

Noah: Well, my uncle runs a restaurant, and I've always known it was what I wanted to do too when I was older. I've helped him at the weekends for a year now and I've seen how running a restaurant is exhausting but enjoyable too because of the responsibility. That side of it can also be quite frightening at times, and I've seen how stressed my uncle can feel. His restaurant is really popular. He gets a lot of repeat business, you know, customers coming back again and again. I think the reason for that is that they're looking for the kind of quality that's not easy to find in most restaurants. In fact, I've seen how hard that is for my uncle to achieve day in and day out. He always says to me that anyone starting a restaurant must realise how essential it is to build a strong team and I'm sure he's right. Without that a business like that can't succeed. The staff are like a family, and everyone has to play their part. Now I'm training as a chef, before I try to cook a dish myself, my uncle gets me to eat a plate of it that he's cooked and work out what the ingredients are. That's the starting point. And he's right. How can you cook something if you can't taste what's in it? It's good fun testing myself that way, too! My uncle is also good at telling all of us when we've done something really well. It's great when he shows us a fantastic review someone's written about the restaurant in a local newspaper or online. My uncle hasn't always been so successful. A few years ago, his restaurant wasn't doing very well. It was full at the weekends but empty during the week. People were only booking it for a celebration of some kind. So he made a few changes, made it more relaxed, so people felt it was somewhere they could go every day of the week. Another thing my uncle insists on is that every customer receives a level of service which never changes, whatever time or day of the week it is. And I've realised that commitment to detail is the way to achieve this. In fact, we hardly ever get any complaints and rarely about the food. But sometimes people aren't happy because they can't get a table. The restaurant is by the river, and we have 40 tables, but in the summer if the weather is good we get over 500 calls a day for reservations. That's about 3,000 calls a week! Demand is really high and we have to make sure that people aren't disappointed when they do get a table. My uncle does that by making sure the menu is always exciting. When I have my own restaurant, it'll be great because I'll be the one to choose what goes on the menu. I'm sure that will never get boring! That's one thing I love about cooking – it's seasonal, so the kind of things we cook changes every three months or so. In summer, it's really light and fresh with lots of fish and salads and more cold food, of course. Then after that, the food starts to get richer and heavier in September. There's more red meat and game on the menu, for example.

Interviewer: Well, Noah, you're obviously very committed and you deserve to succeed. Good luck, and maybe one day I'll be able to come and eat at a restaurant you are running!

Reading and Use of English Part 3

1 movement   2 locally   3 reliable   4 difficulty
5 solution   6 impossible   7 easiest   8 protection

5 Study time

Grammar

1 2 wore   3 helps   4 don't/do not make   5 want   6 are
   7 had   8 need   9 'd/would come   10 'll/will see

Vocabulary

1 2 attend → expect   3 assist → attend   4 know → find out   5 take part in → join   6 know → get to know   7 took part in → attended   8 attend → see

2 2 find out   3 pointed out   4 got away with   5 sort out   6 put off   7 got through   8 turned out

Answer key: Unit 5

3 2 course 3 marks 4 academic 5 degree
6 prospects 7 coursework 8 research 9 tutor
10 tutorials

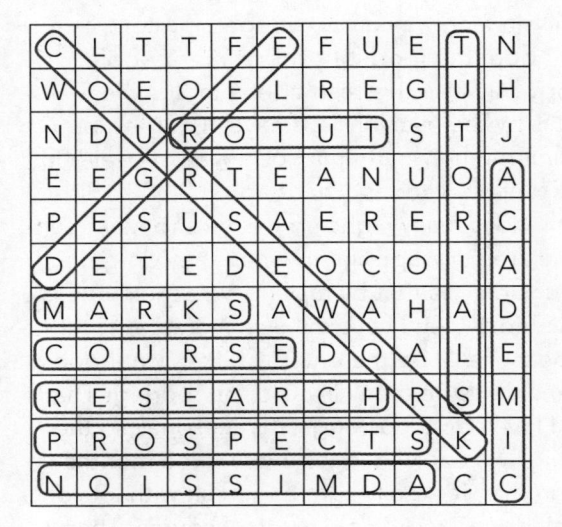

```
C L T T F E F U E T N
W O E O E L R E G U H
N D U R O T U T S T J
E E G R T E A N U O A
P E S U S A E R E R C
D E T E D E O C O I A
M A R K S A W A H A D
C O U R S E D O A L E
R E S E A R C H R S M
P R O S P E C T S K I
N O I S S I M D A C C
```

4 -ation: application, concentration, identification, publication

-ence: existence, difference, preference

-ment: amazement, arrangement, encouragement, punishment

-ance: appearance, assistance, guidance, performance

5 1 publication 2 difference 3 amazement
4 existence 5 assistance

Reading and Use of English Part 6

1 C 2 B 3 D 4 F 5 G 6 A

Listening Part 3

1 C 2 F 3 H 4 A 5 G

▶ Track 06

Speaker 1: Maths is definitely my favourite subject – even though most of my friends say they don't like it because <u>they find it too difficult. It's the opposite for me, in fact</u>. And although the teacher sets us quite a lot of homework, I get that done pretty quickly, really. That's a good thing because my parents can't ever help me: they wish they could remember some of the maths they learned at school, but they can only recall a few fairly basic things. I hope that doesn't happen to me, even though I still have no idea what I want to do when I leave school.

Speaker 2: I like most of my school subjects, but my favourite is geography. My parents are both art teachers, but <u>one of their friends is a geographer specialising in climate research, and I'd like to do something similar myself one day. That makes my geography lessons seem more relevant than all the others, which is why I like the subject best</u>. My teacher has suggested a few books for me to read. I've started one and I'm enjoying finding out more about a topic that isn't covered in much depth in the textbook. My French teacher says if I spent that much time on my French homework, she'd be delighted!

Speaker 3: Most of <u>my friends think that physics is quite a hard subject, but that's what particularly appeals to me. I feel a real sense of achievement when I've managed to work something out on my own</u>, without checking how to do it in the textbook. My parents are proud of me, but they don't understand any of it, so we never talk about it. I just get on with my homework, and if I have to check anything, I tend to use the Internet. I think I might end up studying something I find a bit easier, like music, at university – but I'm still not sure.

Speaker 4: I love English literature. Our teacher makes us write a lot of essays at home, which is time-consuming, but <u>I love discussing what I'm writing about with my mum and dad, and that's why it's my favourite subject</u>, really. I'm reading all sorts of books I wouldn't have read otherwise, which is very interesting. The textbook doesn't help much, but that's OK. Most of my friends are in a different class for English – it's a big school – but that's not a bad thing because our teachers sometimes have different ideas about the books and we can compare notes. We often sit together in the school canteen talking about books!

Speaker 5: I never thought I'd say my favourite subject was chemistry, but it is now. In the past, I struggled in class, and also with my homework, but that's because I just couldn't understand most of it. My parents couldn't help, and my friends were equally confused. I didn't find the textbook much use, either. Then when <u>we got a new teacher last year</u>, I thought it was just going to be the same, but <u>he could really explain things and that just makes him brilliant</u>. Chemistry doesn't seem too hard anymore, though I still need help of course.

Reading and Use of English Part 3

1 effective 2 inhabitants 3 knowledge
4 requirements 5 recommendations
6 possibilities 7 unsuitable 8 memorable

6 My first job

Grammar

1 2 a 3 a 4 the 5 the 6 a 7 a 8 – 9 – 10 a
11 a 12 the 13 a 14 a 15 a 16 the 17 –

2 2 equipment 3 food 4 suitcases 5 information
6 views 7 suggestions 8 dish 9 luggage
10 experience

Vocabulary

1 1 full-time job 2 paid job 3 weekend work
4 temporary job 5 skilled work 6 outdoor work

2 3 occasions ⟶ opportunities 4 an opportunity ⟶ a possibility / a chance 5 funny ⟶ fun 6 ✓
7 ✓ 8 occasion ⟶ opportunity / chance

Writing Part 2

1 2 Although 3 so as a result 4 For the same reason,
5 The disadvantage is that 6 On the other hand,
7 Both 8 If you like,

2 1 He writes about jobs in a supermarket and jobs as a waiter in a restaurant or café.
2 There are jobs available because people prefer not to work in the evening and at weekends.
3 *Suggested paragraph breaks:* After Jay, selling!, waiters, area, enjoy

Listening Part 1

1 B 2 A 3 B 4 C 5 A 6 B 7 A 8 C

▶ Track 07

Presenter: One. You overhear two teenagers talking.
Boy: I'm glad we've nearly finished now! What a day!
Girl: Mine hasn't been too bad, <u>but the kitchen here's not that stressful to work in. You've been dealing with the customers</u>.
Boy: Yeah, but it'll be your turn next Saturday, won't it?
Girl: Yeah, then I'll be exhausted! I'll walk with you to the station if you're ready.
Boy: OK, but I need to stop at the supermarket to get something for my mum.
Girl: Oh, well, if you're nearly ready to leave now, I'll meet you there – I've still got a bit of clearing up to do. I'll see you outside the supermarket entrance in ten minutes.

Presenter: Two. You hear a teenager talking on the phone about a part-time job he has been offered.
Boy: Yeah, they've offered it to me. Well, as soon as I went into the interview I kind of knew I was right for the job, so I was really expecting to be offered it. But now it's actually happened, I've realised that I've got to work every Friday and Saturday evening and <u>I don't know if I really want to. It's quite well paid though so I should take it</u>. In fact, I'm lucky to have been offered it. But then again, something with better hours might come up anytime and it wouldn't look good if I only stayed in this job for a couple of weeks.

Presenter: Three. You hear a girl talking to her teacher about her holiday job.
Girl: Well, being a photographer's assistant is quite varied compared to my friends' holiday jobs and I really enjoyed it. I know some people would find it a bit boring maybe, helping her take photos of children all day long. Some photographers obviously do more fascinating work. The children's parents bring them to the studio and one of the things I do is entertain them while she gets the right shots. <u>But I love it and the day passes so fast because the whole process fascinates me</u> – watching how she gets the right shot and every one is different. I'm on my feet nearly all day but that doesn't bother me.

Presenter: Four. You hear a woman talking to a group of teenagers.
Woman: Welcome everybody. Now, I know you're all interested in a career in engineering so we're very pleased to have you here for a week as work experience. You all filled in a form saying what you are particularly interested in. It's been a bit difficult as the majority of you have asked to be placed in the same department so, <u>to give everybody the same chance, you'll spend a day in each department rather than a week in the same one</u>. If you look in your folder, you will find a map and a list of where you are all starting today. Now are there any …

Answer key: Unit 7

Presenter: Five. You hear two teenagers talking about babysitting.

Boy: I don't mind it, really. I mean compared to some jobs, babysitting's hardly difficult, is it?

Girl: Well, it depends on what sort of kids you're looking after really. Maybe the ones you look after are in bed when you arrive and you get to watch TV all evening. That's easy money. But it isn't usually like that for me!

Boy: No, it isn't for me, either, and I wouldn't say it's very well paid, but <u>I like playing with the kids</u>, don't you?

Girl: I don't have any little brothers or sisters, so sure, <u>I feel the same about that. They can be really cute</u>, can't they?

Presenter: Six. You hear a teenager talking to his boss.

Woman: Peter, you should have been here an hour ago. We need you to help the chef in the kitchen. Was your bus cancelled or something?

Teenager: But I'm early – I don't start for another half an hour. I've come to leave my bag and I'm going to give my mum a hand with the shopping. She dropped me off in the car and now she's gone to the supermarket.

Woman: But you're standing in for Sarah who can't work today. She said she'd ring you.

Teenager: She did but she was so busy telling me where she's going today, <u>she didn't say anything about you needing me to do extra</u>.

Woman: Ohhh …

Presenter: Seven. You hear a message on a telephone answering service.

Man: Hello, Emily. I'm just ringing about tomorrow. I know you don't usually work in the shop on Saturday morning because of your drama group, but there just isn't anyone else this week because of Michael being ill. I've just got your text saying you can work all day and <u>I'm really grateful as I don't know what we would have done – it's really good of you</u>. I'm going to a wedding so you won't be able to contact me but I know you'll manage. Let me know if you'd like a Saturday afternoon off next month instead, or if you'd prefer the extra cash. As soon as Michael is better, we'll be back to normal.

Presenter: Eight. You hear a girl talking to a friend.

Girl: Hi, Colin. You work in that hotel on Sundays, don't you? I really need a job.

Boy: I can check to see if there are any vacancies. I'm learning quite a bit about different recipes. I do all the preparation and I'm getting really fast at chopping veg.

Girl: Mmm … not sure if that would suit me. I'm better at dealing with people.

Boy: Like in the restaurant or <u>the front desk you mean</u>?

Girl: Yeah, but I'm quite clumsy carrying plates and things. <u>I'd really enjoy booking people in and that sort of thing</u> though.

Boy: I'll ask if they need anyone.

Reading and Use of English Part 7

1 C   2 A   3 B   4 D   5 C   6 A   7 B   8 C   9 D   10 A

7 High adventure

Grammar

1 1 going / to go   2 trying   3 to train / training
4 to rest   5 not to go   6 doing / to do   7 to bring
8 continuing   9 visiting   10 to sail / sailing
11 travelling   12 to tell

2 1 allowed   2 decided   3 expected   4 avoided
5 admitted   6 failed   7 thought   8 succeeded

Vocabulary

1 1 take part in   2 took his place   3 take up to
4 take exercise   5 take a risk   6 take turns

2 1 after   2 on   3 off   4 up   5 away   6 to

3 1 watching   2 doing   3 doing   4 hear   5 watch
6 going

Writing Part 2

conviniently ⟶ conveniently
corse ⟶ course
acommodation ⟶ accommodation
confortable ⟶ comfortable
excelent ⟶ excellent
bycycle ⟶ bicycle
wether ⟶ weather
oportunities ⟶ opportunities
wich ⟶ which
belive ⟶ believe

Answer key: Unit 8

Listening Part 2

1 size 2 explorer 3 challenge 4 darkness
5 problem-solving 6 risks / a risk 7 gas 8 training
9 panic 10 confidence

▶ **Track 08**

Cave diving, officially the world's most dangerous sport, isn't for everyone. If you're the kind of person who enjoys being underwater in dark, enclosed spaces then it's probably the ultimate adventure sport. People often say cave diving sounds like their worst nightmare but for people like me it's a real passion. It's like the caves have a power over me. What I love about it most is the amazing beauty of these caves, not to mention their incredible <u>size</u>. It's like nowhere else. You're looking at rock formations that are millions of years old and the water is crystal clear.

Another thing I like is that I'm seeing things that no one has ever seen before; I'm like an <u>explorer</u> discovering new places. This is especially true now that I go down on my own. When I was first learning how to dive, I went down with an instructor who showed me where to go so that wasn't the same. But you shouldn't go alone until you've had lots of practice and experience. Even then it can be very dangerous but that's what some divers say they love about it. They enjoy the <u>challenge</u>. I always plan my dives as much as I can as I prefer to be in control. If I feel stressed, I make mistakes. But if you know what you're doing, then you shouldn't have a problem. I think the worst thing that can happen is if your lights go out for some reason; it's really scary being in total <u>darkness</u>. So that's why it's important to take two sets of lights with you. Something you need to be aware of is that you can't immediately escape to the surface if you get into difficulties, which means your survival depends on your <u>problem-solving</u> abilities. You need to recognise what is happening and follow all the correct procedures you've been taught.

Having said all that, cave diving isn't dangerous if you follow a few simple rules. Most of the accidents you read about could have been avoided if these people had followed simple steps to reduce the <u>risks</u> involved. Usually they've done something which wasn't safe and they should have known better. It's also very important to know when to 'call a dive', or go back. Another big danger is getting lost. Imagine entering an underwater room and looking back to see there is not one, but dozens of passages, and not knowing which way leads back to the entrance. The longer you spend under water, the more <u>gas</u> you need on your back to help you breathe. You need enough to allow you the time to get back to the entrance if something goes wrong. So it's obviously only a sport for experienced divers. Even if you have all the right equipment, that won't help you if you don't know what you're doing so you should never attempt cave diving without adequate <u>training</u>. There are lots of good courses to choose from.

It takes a special sort of person to become a good cave diver. You must be the kind of person who doesn't <u>panic</u> if something goes wrong, and that takes a great deal of self-control. However, you can learn a lot about yourself from diving and I think knowing you can survive in such a demanding environment gives you greater <u>confidence</u>, both at work and socially. It won't help you get a job or make friends but it will make you feel better about yourself.

If you're interested in finding out more, there are a couple of great websites I can recommend …

Reading and Use of English Part 2

1 of 2 be 3 have / need 4 There 5 able
6 Because / Since / As 7 in 8 more / better

Reading and Use of English Part 1

1 B 2 A 3 C 4 B 5 D 6 B 7 D 8 C

8 Dream of the stars

Grammar

1 2 My whole family watched it yesterday and we all liked it.
   3 I've never seen it and I don't want to.
   4 I'm going to watch it next week.
   5 I can't wait for the next episode because I'm really enjoying it.
   6 I've only seen one episode and it was a bit boring but I might watch it again.

2 B warn C complain D promise E announce
  F admit G recommend

Answer key: Unit 8

3 2 the food tasted disgusting.
3 she would/'d give the money back the next day.
4 he was going to live in Brazil.
5 I / we (should/'d) watch the new James Bond film.
6 the city centre could be dangerous at night.
7 she had/'d told a lie.

Vocabulary

1 Across: 1 play   2 public   3 producer
4 contestant   5 scene   7 privacy   10 stage
12 audience   13 location   14 acting   15 series

Down: 1 presenter   2 performance   6 celebrity
8 studios   9 spectators   11 tabloid

2 2 C   3 B   4 A   5 D

Listening Part 3

1 B   2 E   3 A   4 H   5 F

▶ Track 09

Speaker 1: Have you seen *Black Watch 3* yet? I really enjoyed the other *Black Watch* films and this one is just as funny. It's got the same actors in it as the others and they're really good as usual. The story continues from the last film – you know when they were on that desert island – but even if you hadn't seen that, you'd still be able to follow what was happening. But I was just getting involved in the story when it suddenly finished. It's only half the length of the other two films. It started well but didn't get a chance to develop properly.

Speaker 2: I'd read about *The Purple Rose* and it sounded really good. I hadn't heard of any of the actors but they should get a lot more parts now after their performances in this film. The only problem was that there were five or six different storylines which made it very difficult to follow. It's full of action which meant I couldn't take my eyes off the screen, and there are some good comedy scenes, but I wasn't sure half the time why something was happening. It could have been shorter too and it wouldn't have lost anything.

Speaker 3: *A Beautiful Land* is set in New Zealand and is based on a book of the same name. They'd obviously gone to a lot of trouble to make sure they followed the story and the locations in the book. There are lots of beautiful shots. It's about two men who emigrated there a hundred years ago, so it's about their friendship really, and the two main actors are really good. But there's not much else to it and, to be honest, I couldn't wait for it to finish. It could have been at least 30 minutes shorter. It really wouldn't have made much difference.

Speaker 4: Stephen Chadley is my favourite director so I was looking forward to his new film *Out of the Blue*. He always chooses at least one unknown actor as one of the stars and he's never got it wrong before. So, despite being set in a wonderful location in southern Thailand and having a really good script and gripping storyline, I didn't think any of the actors did a very good job, even those who are quite well-known. There were some funny moments though and it's got a very good ending – not what you'd expect at all.

Speaker 5: Jack Bradley and Manuel Gonzalez star in *A Long Ride*. They are apparently good friends in real life. That came across in the film which is about a trip on a motorbike across South America. They didn't have a script – they just filmed what happened and a lot of interesting things did happen! The acting was of a really high standard but they are both very good comic actors and it was a shame they didn't take advantage of that – it could have been quite funny if they had. Although it was quite long, because they're always moving on to a new location, it didn't seem to matter.

Reading and Use of English Part 4

1 me to go   2 for not coming / having come   3 Tom of scratching / having scratched   4 my sister to lend me
5 about our room being   6 her (that) there was

Reading and Use of English Part 6

1 C   2 F   3 E   4 A   5 G   6 B

… Answer key: Unit 9

9 Secrets of the mind

Grammar

1 2 She could / might / may be working too hard.
3 He might not / may not / can't (NB NOT could not) like it any more.
4 That must be quite good fun.
5 That can't be Claire's little sister.
6 He must have got some money for his birthday.
7 They can't have had another argument.
8 We may / might / could have met before.
9 She can't have learnt/learned it at school.
10 She may / might / could have thought he'd be angry.

2 1 must   2 may   3 might   4 must   5 could

Writing Part 2

1 1 A   2 B   3 old-fashioned, critical, shocked, angry, responsible   4 B

2 1 confident, shy, stressed, upset, competitive, grateful
2 All can be used in 1, 2, 4 & 6; 3 really, (an) extremely, (you can say *quite a big influence*);
5 quite, really, extremely

Vocabulary

1 1 stay   2 pass   3 spend   4 spend   5 staying
6 passed

2 *make:* progress, trouble, peace, an effort, changes, a mistake
cause: confusion, trouble, damage, offence, unhappiness
have: fun, patience, a shock, an impact on

3 1 C   2 E   3 B   4 A   5 D   6 F

4 1 B   2 C   3 F   4 E   5 A   6 D

5 creative, adventurous, nervous

Listening Part 4

1 B   2 C   3 C   4 C   5 A   6 C   7 B

▶ Track 10

Interviewer: My guest this morning is Professor Martin Jackson from the Weller Institute, who's been doing some research into scientific studies on happiness. Welcome to the programme.

Professor: Thank you.

Interviewer: Is happiness something that can really be measured scientifically?

Professor: Oh, very much so. It's something psychologists have been studying for decades. Worldwide surveys have given us a very clear picture of how satisfied people in different countries are with their lives, and we've discovered that simply by asking people how happy they are, we get a measure of happiness that is as good as any that measure different aspects of people's lives, for example, how well off people are. What's new is that, in the same way that wealth is used to measure government success, we expect that within ten years, governments will be judged on how happy they have made us.

Interviewer: That's very interesting. So individual happiness can really have an impact on society?

Professor: Yes. Some studies have shown that happy people live longer than other people. The difference can be as much as nine years between the happiest and unhappiest groups, which is very significant if you consider that a good diet has been shown to only increase life expectancy by an average of five or six years. That's probably not what most people expect to hear as we're told so much about the importance of diet.

Interviewer: That is quite surprising. Do the studies show if people are getting happier?

Professor: Interestingly, happiness levels have remained stable in industrialised countries for the last 50 years, despite dramatic increases in the standard of living. So, being richer isn't making us happier, although being poor does make people unhappy. But once you have enough money for a home, food and education, extra money doesn't affect happiness.

Interviewer: So it's true that money can't buy happiness?

Professor: Well, we think that what happens when people buy things they think will make them happy, whether that's a new phone or a bar of chocolate, is that the happiness they get from these things doesn't last. And so they need to buy more to get another short burst of pleasure.

71

Answer key: Unit 10

Interviewer: I see. So I suppose what really makes people happy are their relationships with others.

Professor: Yes. This is the most important key to happiness. And it's the quality of those relationships that counts. So having one or two close friends is just as beneficial for happiness as having a wide circle of family and friends. It's even been suggested that friendship can protect against illness, and that continues throughout our lives.

Interviewer: Really? What about school? Is that important as far as happiness is concerned?

Professor: Indeed it is. We've always known that people are happier when they are busy doing something than sitting around doing nothing, and it goes without saying that people will feel happier if they actually enjoy what they're studying at school or college. But what we're discovering now is that having things to aim for, which develop our skills and abilities, so that we reach our full potential, is essential for our happiness.

Interviewer: I suppose that makes sense. So is there a magic formula for happiness? I mean, is there anything people can do to make themselves happy?

Professor: Well, this is something that psychologists are trying to find out. There are action points which include things like smiling more and being helpful to other people, but there's no hard evidence yet that these things significantly improve happiness. What we do know, however, is that the biggest barrier to happiness is envy. So if we can try not to judge ourselves against other people, we'd certainly be happier.

Interviewer: Well, that sounds like really sound advice. Thank you very much. And if you've got any questions for Professor Jackson …

Reading and Use of English Part 3

1 psychological   2 combinations   3 Comparisons
4 preference   5 typically   6 response   7 surroundings
8 behaviour

Reading and Use of English Part 2

1 has   2 at / into   3 on   4 which   5 when   6 be
7 or   8 much / often

10 On the money

Grammar

1 2 wasn't able to / couldn't   3 can   4 haven't been able to   5 was able to / could   6 Will you be able to
7 was able to   8 can usually / is usually able to

2 3 as → like
7 like → as
8 as → like / such as
10 like → as

Vocabulary

1 2 arrive   3 get   4 reached   5 arrived   6 reach

2 2 brands   3 sale   4 bargains   5 chain
6 competitors   7 guarantee   8 refund   9 stock
10 counter

3 2 in   3 out   4 away   5 out of   6 out   7 into
8 back   9 without   10 up

Reading and Use of English Part 6

1 B   2 G   3 D   4 A   5 E   6 F

Listening Part 1

1 B   2 A   3 C   4 B   5 C   6 B   7 A   8 C

▶ Track 11

Presenter: One. You hear a woman talking to her son.

Woman: I'm happy for you to go on holiday with your friends and I'm sure you'll have a good time. I know you need some pocket money though and it really isn't going to help you if I give you money every time you need it. You already have your allowance – I don't know where that's all gone. It would be a good idea for you to earn some money by getting a weekend job. You've got time to save up. Then you might be more careful with it when you've got more idea of the value. So it's up to you to make a decision now.

Presenter: Two. You overhear a teenager talking to a shop assistant.

Teenager: I bought this jacket last week and I really like it. I didn't have time to try it on so I took it home with me and tried it on there but it's too small. I'm afraid <u>I'll have to ask you for my money back</u>. There isn't anything else here that I want at the moment or I could have exchanged it. I could try a bigger one but they really look much too big and also they're not in the colour I want. I've got it here in the bag.

Presenter: Three. You overhear two people talking.

Boy: I'm working all day on Saturday because it's going to be really busy apparently.

Girl: Me too, but I need the money so I don't mind. I hope I get to be in the stock room rather than being on the till. People are in such a rush at the weekend.

Boy: Yeah, and some people just come in for a newspaper and they have to stand in a long queue.

Girl: <u>And they can be really rude sometimes even though it's not our fault</u>. It isn't fair – they should think about what it's like for us.

Boy: Oh, I just ignore them. They're being ridiculous.

Presenter: Four. You hear the following on the radio.

Man: ... that's certainly been very informative and if anyone would like more information on any of the topics we've discussed, it's all on our website, www.looknorth.com. Before we move on to our weekly programme, *On the Coast*, I need to remind you that The Deer, the popular Australian rock band, are playing at the City Hall on Friday. <u>Tickets go on sale this afternoon, and they'll sell out quickly, so I'd get down there as soon as you can if you're a fan.</u> If I didn't have to be here, I'd certainly get down there myself. And now, we join Mark Priestley who's out and about ...

Presenter: Five. You hear two people talking about their holiday plans.

Man: Shall I get some foreign currency from the bank for our trip?

Woman: We could do it at the airport.

Man: But you get poor exchange rates there. I'll check it out on the Internet. <u>I've bought one of these body belts so I can put my money in it</u>. I know some people think they're a waste of time.

Woman: <u>Oh, I use one of those – I prefer it to having a bag</u>. Let's not change too much money. We can always get more cash when we get there.

Man: But we're not going to be near many towns and we don't want to run out – better to have a bit extra.

Presenter: Six. You overhear a woman talking to a friend.

Woman: I bought a new computer yesterday. A young man showed me what they had in the shop – everything has changed so much since I last bought one. <u>He couldn't do enough for me</u> – checking out what I asked him. But it took forever because he had to keep looking everything up and he didn't go about it in a very logical way. He came up with all the answers in the end but he didn't seem to know much more than me. But I was really pleased with what I got thanks to his efforts. It was just lucky I wasn't in a hurry.

Presenter: Seven. You hear a teenager talking to his friend about buying clothes online.

Girl: Hi, James. Those are nice jeans.

Boy: They just came in the post. I got them from a website which specialises in this style of jeans.

Girl: Oh, I prefer looking round the shops and trying things on.

Boy: I do too, but on the Internet you can compare all the different sites – lots of them have the same thing on them – <u>then you know you're really getting a bargain</u>.

Girl: I find there's so much to choose from on the Internet I don't know where to start.

Boy: I know. That's why I usually find what I want in the shops and then get it online.

Presenter: Eight. You hear a message on an answerphone.

Boy: I'd love to come climbing with you but the thing is I haven't got any of the gear and it costs a lot to hire it. My brother has everything I need but he won't lend it to me even if I ask him nicely. I was telling my granny and she said it was a real shame that I can't go, so she's going to talk to my brother. He adores Granny and she can usually persuade him to do something. So, <u>I'm pretty hopeful</u> but if he says no, there aren't any other options. I'll have to come with you when you do something else.

Reading and Use of English Part 3

1 choice 2 unknown 3 reasonable 4 similarities
5 surprising 6 actually 7 sensible 8 effective

Answer key: Unit 11

11 Medical matters

Grammar

1 a 2 which   3 whose   4 which   5 whose
6 which   7 which   8 who   9 which   10 where

b 5 The government, whose job it is to promote healthy eating, is not doing enough to encourage parents to change their shopping and cooking habits.
7 Childhood obesity, which is now a huge problem in Europe, may have a significant impact on life expectancy.

c 1, 2, 4, 6, 8, 9

d Relative pronouns can be omitted from sentences 4 and 9.

2 1 D   2 F   3 A   4 C   5 B   6 E

Vocabulary

1 satisfaction   willingness   helpfulness
awareness   patience   ability   experience
convenience   accuracy   security   certainty
happiness   honesty

2 *able* has two negative forms: disabled, unable
dis: dissatisfied, disabled, dishonest
im: impossible, impatient
in: inexperienced, inconvenient, inaccurate, insecure
un: unwilling, unhelpful, unaware, unable, uncertain, unhappy

Writing Part 1

2 1 F   2 C   3 H   4 B   5 G   6 E   7 A

Reading and Use of English Part 3

1 treatment   2 strength   3 fitness   4 inexperienced
5 active   6 additional   7 balanced   8 healthy

Reading and Use of English Part 4

1 advised me to do more   2 if you don't stop
3 suggested going / that we go   4 must have eaten more vegetables   5 explained (that) he / she would
6 was too tired to

Listening Part 4

1 C   2 B   3 B   4 C   5 A   6 C   7 B

▶ Track 12

Jake: Thank you for seeing me, Doctor Reid. I've got some questions I need to investigate for my project on the effect of sleep on school students.

Dr Reid: OK. Well, fire away!

Jake: Well, the first thing I'm not sure about is whether people in general are sleeping less than in the past. I've read some reports on the Internet which give conflicting information.

Dr Reid: It's good to see you are checking your facts; the Internet can be unreliable. As you know, <u>today the average person gets about seven and a half hours' sleep every night</u>, which is a bit less than the recommended eight hours. However, <u>without the interference of electric light bulbs and alarm clocks, people usually sleep for nine hours and this was the case up to the early part of the 20th century</u>.

Jake: I thought so. And is it natural for people to just sleep at night like most people do now?

Dr Reid: If allowed to, we would sleep for two periods in the night and get up and do things in the middle. We just don't do that now because of our working days. Also, most people have a tendency to feel sleepy <u>after lunch</u> but because of the way our days are structured, most of us just have a cup of coffee and carry on, when <u>we should let ourselves have a nap</u> – just for half an hour at the most. But a constant need to nap is a sign that people aren't getting enough sleep at night, which is a problem that seems to be getting worse.

Jake: I've read that it's a problem that affects teenagers in particular.

Dr Reid: That's correct. A lot of teenagers are getting far too little sleep and there are concerns that this could have a serious long-term impact on their health, but we don't know for sure yet. Researchers are also looking into how far a lack of sleep affects young people with depression. But one study has clearly demonstrated that <u>high-school students getting low grades also get on average one hour less sleep than students getting As and Bs</u>.

Jake: Really? Why do you think teenagers aren't getting enough sleep?

Dr Reid: It's an interesting question. It's a problem that seems to affect all teenagers, not just the ones who eat the wrong things and who don't take any exercise. <u>So my feeling is that parents need to take more responsibility.</u> Too many teenagers watch TV in their rooms or play computer games until very late, or they're allowed to go out on school nights.

Jake: Some of my friends say they stay up late because they can't get to sleep if they go to bed earlier.

Dr Reid: Well, there are things you can do to make yourself feel sleepy. Your brain needs to switch off and relax so don't have any drinks that contain caffeine, which includes hot chocolate and a lot of soft drinks. <u>Reading a book you know well</u> or listening to a story, rather than music, should help your brain to relax.

Jake: So you shouldn't do your homework just before going to sleep?

Dr Reid: Definitely not! Schools should be careful how much homework they set because working late in the evening doesn't help people to get a good night's sleep. It would be better for schools to stay open for longer so that pupils can do their homework before they get home to avoid this problem. Another thing that some schools have tried successfully is to <u>begin the school day half an hour later, which seems like a good idea to me.</u>

Jake: Well, that's very interesting. Thank you, Doctor Reid. Just one last question. Is it true that our brains are actively thinking while we're asleep?

Dr Reid: Well, our brains are good at sorting information while we are asleep. <u>It's often the case that we wake up having found the answer to a problem that we'd been worrying about the day before.</u> But it's important to write it down immediately as we can forget it easily.

Jake: Great. Thanks very much for your help.

Answer key: Unit 12

12 Animal kingdom

Grammar

1 2 had started, would have driven   3 had run, would have caught   4 hadn't gone, wouldn't have seen   5 hadn't missed, wouldn't have noticed   6 had been, wouldn't have been

2 2 hope   3 wish   4 hope   5 hope   6 wish   7 wish   8 hope   9 wish   10 wish

3 2b I wish the elephants ~~had~~ come closer. → would
4b If we ~~had~~ made a lot of noise, we would have seen more animals. → hadn't

Vocabulary

1 prevent   2 check   3 avoid   4 supervised   5 control   6 protect

Writing Part 2

1 1 B or C   2 D or E   3 B or C   4 D or E   5 A

2 *Suggested answers*
1 1B or 3B   2 5A   3 2E or 4E   4 2D or 4D   5 1C

Reading and Use of English Part 5

1 B   2 C   3 D   4 B   5 A   6 D

Listening Part 2

1 a degree   2 contact   3 public speaking
4 routine(s)   5 boat   6 smell (of fish)
7 negative   8 communicate   9 films   10 14/fourteen

▶ **Track 13**

Kirsty: Good morning. My name's Kirsty Willis and I'm here to talk to you about what it's like to work in a zoo and about some other careers you may be interested in that also involve working with animals.

OK. The job that most people associate with working with animals is in a zoo. Although there are job openings which don't require many qualifications, for most posts there's a lot of competition so it's unlikely that you'll be considered without <u>a degree</u>. Zoos have changed a lot over the years and focus on a conservation role nowadays which involves care, education and study. But don't expect to have very much <u>contact</u> with the animals because they tend to be left as much as possible to live as they would in the wild. Although you still may help with normal tasks of feeding, keeping records, etc., a lot of the time is spent on education, so you should have excellent <u>public-speaking</u> skills. You'll be talking to visitors at the zoo and showing groups of schoolchildren round, so you need to be able to get your enthusiasm across to them. Because what happens in a zoo is more or less the same each day, the job will appeal to you if you like to have <u>routines</u> in your life. You will have to deal with unexpected problems and challenges on occasions of course, but that's the same in most jobs.

Another related area is working in aquariums with sea mammals and fish. You need similar skills to those required for working in a zoo but you also need to be able to swim well and have experience of using a <u>boat</u> as most of the aquariums have large areas of water. You'll spend a large part of the day preparing and distributing the fishy diets, and dealing with chemicals that are used in the tanks. The job isn't as physically tiring as working in a zoo but by the time you go home, you will almost certainly <u>smell</u>. It will be obvious to everyone that you've been working with fish!

One job that immediately springs to mind when we mention working with animals is working as a vet. Training for this takes a long time, as long or even longer than for a doctor. You can work with all kinds of animals but you have to take into consideration that it can be frustrating because the animals can be very <u>negative</u> towards the vet. Conditioning tells them that every time this guy comes around, they aren't feeling well or it's going to be an uncomfortable, scary experience. To be a good vet, you don't just need knowledge of the science, you should be able to <u>communicate</u> with both animals and humans. That skill is really important – much more than making a quick decision about what is wrong with an animal.

The last job I'm going to talk about is being an animal trainer. There used to be opportunities in circuses but animals are used much less now to perform, but animals trainers are still required in <u>films</u> so it's worth thinking about that. The training required is primarily experience. The pay for these jobs can be pretty low and many people will work for free at first.

It's also very hard work. The day starts early, as early as four or five in the morning and in most cases won't finish till <u>14</u> hours later. Don't forget in most jobs you work eight hours a day maximum. This is definitely not a nine to five job!

If you'd like any more information, there are a number of websites that will …

13 House space

Grammar

1 a
2 She wants to have / get the windows cleaned.
3 She is going to have / get the hedge cut.
4 She would like to have / get the rubbish removed.
5 She thinks she should have / get the gate replaced.
b
7 She has had / got the windows cleaned.
8 She has had / got the hedge cut.
9 She has had / got the rubbish removed.
10 She has had / got the gate replaced.

2 2 needn't have bought   3 won't let me have
4 don't have to   5 can't   6 shouldn't have   7 were supposed to   8 Don't let your little brother   9 must
10 are allowed to

3 1 on   2 in / at   3 on   4 on   5 at   6 in   7 in   8 at

Vocabulary

Options which are not correct
2 likeable   3 installed   4 gives an overview of
5 convenient   6 richly   7 poor   8 well equipped
9 place   10 area

Listening Part 4

1 B   2 B   3 C   4 A   5 C   6 A   7 B

Answer key: Unit 13

Track 14

Matt: Hello and welcome to the programme. This morning we're going to discuss 'boomerang kids': adults that stay at home or return after university to live with their parents until they're in their mid-twenties or even their mid-thirties. And here to tell us about the results of a recent survey on this subject is Sadie Andrews.

Sadie: Thanks, Matt. Yes. Well, the results show that the number of 18- to 24-year-olds in Europe still living at home has reached 67%, although that figure is much lower for countries in northern Europe – <u>Sweden has overtaken the UK and France as the country with the fewest 'boomerang kids'</u>, with only 46% of this age-group still living at home. As you might expect, that figure rises to over 90% for countries in southern Europe such as Spain and Italy, where young people have traditionally lived with their parents for longer. And despite relatively low rents, there's little change here because <u>family relationships remain very strong</u>.

Matt: That's very interesting. And what about outside Europe?

Sadie: Yes. The survey also covered the United States where the trend is also for people to live at home longer, though here the reason given wasn't to do with people having to pay back huge student loans, as this is nothing new. 'Boomerang kids' here said there was <u>no reason for them to leave home because they got on so well with their parents</u>. Many people reported continuing to live at home even after they got married. So there's obviously less of a generation gap than there used to be.

Matt: I can see there are advantages. Having your mum to do your washing and ironing, for example.

Sadie: People interviewed for the survey didn't admit to that – even if it were true – though I know my mum wouldn't be prepared to do my washing and ironing. In fact, the impression I get is that boomerang kids are pretty responsible people. What they seem to <u>appreciate most is that they're not spending vast sums of money on rent and other bills so they can put money aside for when they do leave</u>. But of course, there are disadvantages. Interviewees report that having to tell their parents what time they'll be home or not being able to spend time at home with friends without first asking permission is a frustrating experience and <u>they complain that a lot of parents still think of 'boomerang kids' as just kids</u>.

Matt: Yes. That must be difficult. What about the parents? What do they think?

Sadie: On the whole, most don't seem to mind and are willing to help their adult children out wherever possible. However, in some cases parents find that just when they've reached the point in their lives when they have the time and the money to do whatever they want, <u>they are held back because of their adult children's needs</u>. On the other hand, there is evidence to show that having boomerang kids back at home does keep them young – they're more likely to be in touch with the latest ideas in fashion and watch different TV programmes. And some parents say they feel less tired because there's more going on at home – maybe their children's friends coming in and more people to talk to.

Matt: Right. So, before we hear from the listeners, what advice would you give for families in this situation?

Sadie: Well, obviously things are going to run more smoothly if everyone involved does their fair share, so it's a good idea to work out a fair contribution for bills and jobs such as shopping and washing-up. However, feedback from the results of the survey suggests that <u>deciding in advance how often they are going to eat together, if at all, and at what time, will avoid resentment building up on both sides. This causes more arguments than any other issue</u>.

Matt: Thanks, Sadie.

Writing Part 2

1 1 F 2 E 3 B 4 A 5 C 6 D

2 1, 2 and 4

Reading and Use of English Part 1

1 A 2 D 3 C 4 A 5 B 6 D 7 C 8 B

14 Fiesta!

Grammar

1 2 is organised   3 is given   4 has been raised
5 were awarded   6 was chosen   7 is hoped
8 will be offered / are offered   9 was formed
10 be seen   11 are already being made / have already been made   12 to be added

2 2 It is thought that a new waterpark will probably be built next year.   3 It is reported that the new team has been selected.   4 Federer is considered to be the best tennis player ever.   5 Chocolate is reported to be good for your brain.   6 It is believed that the bones found on the beach belonged to a dinosaur.

Writing Part 1

1 2 It   3 them   4 this/it   5 these   6 them   7 this/it
8 those

2 Suggestion
Students having the opportunity to show off their musical talent.

3 Paragraph 1: introduction
Paragraph 2: advantages
Paragraph 3: disadvantages
Paragraph 4: conclusion

A recommendation would not usually be found in an essay, but used in a review – suggesting people should read a book or see a film, for example. A description might be found in a story, an article, a review, or possibly in a letter.

4 *Sample answer*

Many schools have drama classes, and some teachers may direct plays, for example, that students can act in. However, should such activities be run by the students themselves?

First of all, being involved in setting up and managing an event is a useful and interesting thing to do. It allows students to gain new skills and learn how to get along together. Furthermore, drama events like plays not only provide opportunities for people to act, but also for others to try out things such as making costumes, painting scenery or designing posters to advertise the event. People of all ages and abilities can help with these.

It could also be argued, though, that most students have too little experience to organise anything so complicated, and that teachers should take responsibility for this type of activity. This also ensures that everyone has a chance to participate, including people who may be shy and quiet and need encouragement to do so.

In conclusion, I think that the best solution is for teachers to organise events. They should take the students' ideas and suggestions into account, but an adult should be in charge.

Vocabulary

1 electrician   politician   <u>photographer</u>   musician
2 <u>accountant</u>   pharmacist   psychologist   economist
3 <u>fisherman/woman</u>   entertainer   banker   supporter
4 lecturer   producer   manufacturer   <u>investigator</u>
5 historian   librarian   <u>sportsman/woman/person</u>   comedian
6 contestant   inhabitant   assistant   <u>employee/employer</u>

Listening Part 3

1 B   2 H   3 G   4 C   5 D

Track 15

Speaker 1: It's going to be good fun: we'll all get together after school in my cousin's flat, and get it ready for the party. Then we'll wait until Louisa arrives. We'll have a cake, and there'll be three candles on it: one for every year she and her family have been away. There'll be piles of food, too, of course, but we'll need it for all the people who are coming. <u>I can't believe I'm going to see her again after all this time – it's definitely worth celebrating!</u> She can't possibly have any idea of what we're planning. We've all promised to keep it secret. I can't wait!

Speaker 2: We always do this, which is nice, because it means having a little celebration at the beginning, rather than the end of the school year. <u>It's a nice way to welcome a person who's after all going to be quite important in our lives for a while. And it's an opportunity for them to get to know the students they'll be teaching.</u> Someone usually bakes a cake and brings it in – it's never me, because my cakes could hardly be called prize-winning – they're usually rather flat! Then we just chat and enjoy this more informal occasion, before getting on with all the work we have to do.

Speaker 3: All my friends took part, though none of us really expected to get anywhere at all. But <u>my best friend had an email back from the organisers saying her short story would be in the final</u>, so you can imagine how excited we all got. Then <u>when she came first, we just had to mark the occasion!</u> My brother passed his driving test last year, so he drove some of us to the beach – other people got lifts, too. Then we had the most wonderful picnic – it was a bit like the birthday parties my brothers and I used to have when we were little. It was lovely!

Speaker 4: All my family are delighted, and my brother is, obviously, so we're all going out to a restaurant to celebrate. That's the best thing for me, though I'm really happy about his success, too. It's very competitive – loads of people want to <u>study at that college</u> because the teaching is so good, apparently. <u>Anyway, he did very well to get in, and that's why my parents are making such a fuss.</u> All his hard work has finally paid off, and he has the whole summer to relax now, because it's the end of term, too. He'll have time to do things like learn to drive – lucky him.

Speaker 5: Although we're all sad my sister's going and we'll miss her a lot, it isn't as if we won't see her loads in the future. <u>She's only going to live a few streets away, and although our flat is much bigger than the one she's moving to, she'll have room for visitors – as long as we don't all go round at once!</u> So we're having the party at our place instead of hers, and we want it to be a happy occasion, naturally. Most of her friends can make it, which is cool, and I'm going to be in charge of the music. I'm really looking forward to it!

Reading and Use of English Part 7

1 A 2 B 3 D 4 E 5 C 6 A 7 C 8 B 9 E 10 D

Acknowledgements

This product is informed by the English Vocabulary Profile, built as part of English Profile, a collaborative programme designed to enhance the learning, teaching and assessment of English worldwide. Its main funding partners are Cambridge University Press and Cambridge Assessment and its aim is to create a 'profile' for English linked to the Common European Framework of Reference for Languages (CEF). English Profile outcomes, such as the English Vocabulary Profile, will provide detailed information about the language that learners can be expected to demonstrate at each CEF level, offering a clear benchmark for learners' proficiency. For more information, please visit www.englishprofile.org

Development of this publication has made use of the Cambridge English Corpus (CEC). The CEC is a computer database of contemporary spoken and written English, which currently stands at over one billion words. It includes British English, American English and other varieties of English. It also includes the Cambridge Learner Corpus, developed in collaboration with Cambridge English Language Assessment. Cambridge University Press has built up the CEC to provide evidence about language use that helps to produce better language teaching materials.

The authors and publisher acknowledge the following sources of copyright material and are grateful for the permissions granted. While every effort has been made, it has not always been possible to identify the sources of all the material used, or to trace all copyright holders. If any omissions are brought to our notice, we will be happy to include the appropriate acknowledgements on reprinting.

The publisher has used its best endeavours to ensure that the URLs for external websites referred to in this book are correct and active at the time of going to press. However, the publisher has no responsibility for the websites and can make no guarantee that a site will remain live or that the content is or will remain appropriate.

Text
p. 7: Joanna Moorhead for the article 'Being an only child' *The Guardian* 4 March 2006. Reproduced by permission of Joanna Moorhead; p. 10: Concord Monitor for the listening exercise 'Chess isn't like life' by Tim Lytvinenko from Concord Monitor, 2 October 2006. Reproduced with permission; p. 22: The Nemours Foundation/KidsHealth for the adapted article 'Going Away to Camp'. Copyright © The Nemours Foundation/KidsHealth. Reprinted with permission; p. 30: Mountain Tracks for the article 'What is ski touring?' from www.mountaintracks.co.uk. Reproduced by permission of Mountain Tracks; p. 35: Adapted article 'Teens can make it all happen' by Judy Gerstel which appeared in The Globe and Mail 13.09.2013. Copyright © Judy Gerstel. Reprinted with permission; p. 39: BBC for the text 'Personality Types' Reproduced by permission of the BBC. http://www.bbc.co.uk/science/humanbody; p. 39: The Press Association for the article 'Happiest day of the year' by Antony Stone, published in *The Independent* 23 June 2006. Courtesy of The Press Association; p. 42: BBC News Online for the text 'Who's Playing Mind Games with you'? Reproduced by permission of BBC News at bbc.co.uk/news; p. 50: Gecko Publishing for the text 'African Safari' from 'Undying teen appeal, it is a safari' by Martin Symington from http://www.travelafricamag.com. Reproduced by permission of Gecko Publishing; p. 55: A L Kennedy for the article 'A Writer's Room' from http://books.guardian.co.uk. Reproduced by permission of A L Kennedy.

Photos
Key: tl = top left; tr = top right; bl = bottom left; br = bottom right
p. 4: Tetra Images/Superstock; p. 6: Blend Images/Alamy; p. 7 (A): joSon/Getty Images; p. 7 (B): MIXA/Alamy; p. 7 (C): Zubin Shroff/Getty Images; p. 7 (D): Alezander Benz/Zefa/Corbis; p. 7 (E): Siri Stafford/Getty Images; p. 8 (bl): Stephan Hoerold/Getty Images; p. 8 (t): iStockphoto/Thinkstock; p. 8 (br): Rob Walls/Alamy; p. 10: ollyy/Shutterstock; p. 11: Barry Lewis/Alamy; p. 12: Jon Arnold Images Ltd/Alamy; p. 14: martovskiy.ru/Getty Images; p. 15 Robert Harding World Imagery/Alamy; p. 18: Edmund Sumner/VIEW Pictures; p. 19: Alison Hancock/Shutterstock; p. 22: iStockphoto/Thinkstock; p. 24: ©W.Disney/Everett/Rex Features; p. 25: moodboard/Alamy; p. 26: Digital Vision/Thinkstock; p. 27: imagebroker.net/Superstock; p. 28: Steve Mason/Photodisc/Thinkstock; p. 29: Anthony West/Corbis; p. 30 (tl): Dan Burton/Alamy; p. 30 (br): Aurora Photos/Alamy; p. 31: LOOK Die Bildagentur der Fotografen GmbH / Alamy; p. 32: iStockphoto/Thinkstock; p. 33: Retna/Photoshot; p. 34: Emmanuel Faure/Getty Images; p. 35: ZUMA Press, Inc./Alamy; p. 38 (tl): George Dolgikh/Shutterstock; p. 38 (b): Digital Vision/Thinkstock; p. 38 (tr): iStockphoto/Thinkstock; p. 39 (tr): iStockphoto/Thinkstock; p. 39 (bl): Ambrophoto/Shutterstock; p. 41 (b): Photononstop/SuperStock; p. 41 (t): michaeljung/Shutterstock; p. 42: Iain Sarjeant/Alamy; p. 46: Tetra Images/Alamy; p. 47: Phil Boorman/Getty Images; p. 49: Miguel Angel Muñor Pellicer/Alamy; p. 50: iStockphoto/Thinkstock; p. 51: Imagebroker/FLPA; p. 53: iStockphoto/Thinkstock; p. 54: EWA Stock/Superstock; p. 55: Unlisted Images/Corbis; p. 56: Robert Convery/Alamy; p. 57: fStop/Alamy; p. 58: Pete M. Wilson/Alamy; p. 59 (tl): David Robertson/Alamy; p. 59 (bl): Dinodia Photos/Alamy; p. 59 (tr): Horizon International Images Ltd/Alamy; p. 59 (br): Patrick Lin/AFP/Getty Images.

Cover image: biletskiy/Shutterstock.

Illustration acknowledgements
Jeff Anderson (Graham-Cameron Illustration) p. 20: Moreno Chiacchiera (Beehive Illustration) p. 48: Roger Harris (NB Illustration) p. 52: Dusan Pavlic (Beehive Illustration) p. 40.

The publishers are grateful to the following contributors:
Sarah Brierley: editorial work
Eleanor Davison: proofreader
Kevin Brown: picture research
Leon Chambers: audio producer
Mark Oliver: sound engineer

Designed and typeset by emc design ltd.
Audio recorded at Soundhouse Studios, London